Contents

CONTENTS

viii

Preface

Long before books existed as physical objects, storytellers handed down to successive generations essential data in narrative form—as in *The Odyssey*, for example, with its advice to seamen and husbands, or the moral and practical wisdom of the books of the Old Testament and similar tribal lore. Even before language existed in our sense at all, stories must have been told by rhythmic gesture accompanied by meaningful phonemes to the beat of stone upon stone or to the sound of hollowed logs used as drums, by breath amplified by passage through the horns of animals, and by plucked strings: ancestral operas. Musical utterance—verse —is the earliest literary technology, easily stored in the mind and chanted as children still chant their alphabets and numbers. By the dawn of our literate civilization the new technology of writing meant that stories no longer had to be memorized collectively as verse but could be written down. Thus stories were stored for future use as prose; but even prose with its regular punctuation reflects its musical origins.

Written language is a recent technology in the long history of our species. It evolved as far as we know and as common sense suggests from counting, keeping score: a commercial activity. The ancient traders of the Near East numbered their bags of grain and flasks of wine with slashes accompanied by pictographs incised or scored upon tablets of clay and stone and presumably also upon wooden boards. Twenty such incisions are still called a score, and scorekeepers still keep score on boards. These scored incisions, the ancestors of adjectives and nouns, were the origin of written language. Eventually, pictographs, reduced to their phonemes—alpha, beta, and so on—became alphabets, and some five hundred years ago this powerful technology was greatly amplified by the invention of movable type, which in its European version gave birth to the Reformation, the Enlightenment, the scientific and industrial revolutions, and the societies that resulted: in other words, our present world with all its wonders and woes. Books in which stories were stored for future use could now be carried to the ends of the earth and would eventually become the stock in trade of bookstores.

In the past dozen years movable type has been replaced by technologies that were unimaginable when I entered the book business in the 1950s. Like the technologies of oral and written language and of movable type, these electronic technologies will radically change the way information is transmitted, stories are read, and cultures are formed. Book publishing in the next ten or twenty years will be very different from the quaint trade that I entered fifty years ago.

Technologies change the world but human nature remains the same. If this were not so, such best-sellers as *The Iliad*, The Psalms of David, and *Beowulf* would be unintelligible to us today. The successive technologies of language, writing, and movable type have put increasingly powerful tools in the hands of storytellers, tools whose uses could not have been imagined when these technologies were new. It will be for our children and their children to learn the meaning of the electronic technologies that are now on the horizon. The book business as I have known it is already obsolete, but the defining human art of storytelling will survive the evolution of cultures and their institutions as it always has. New technologies change the world but they do not erase the past or alter the genome.

Books as physical objects will not pass away to be replaced by electronic signals read from glowing, hand-held screens. Nor will bookstores vanish. But they will coexist hereafter with a vast multilingual directory of digitized texts, assembled from a multitude of sources, perhaps "tagged" for easy reference, and distributed electronically. From this directory readers at their home computers may transfer the materials they select to machines capable of printing and binding single copies on demand at innumerable remote sites and perhaps eventually within their own homes. One such location might be a kiosk at the corner of my Manhattan street while readers at the headwaters of the Nile or in the foothills of the Himalayas will have similar access to the world's wisdom from their own nearby kiosks. The appropriate technology, in embryo, is already at hand and I have seen it. The future that it implies cannot be evaded. I await it with wonder and trepidation.

This book is an expanded version of three lectures that I delivered in October 1999 at the New York Public Library, sponsored by the Center for Scholars and Writers there. I am grateful to Peter Gay, director of the center, and to Paul Leclerc, president of the library, for inviting me to inaugurate this series of lectues and to Peter for having read and improved this manuscript. I am especially grateful to my good friend Barbara Goldsmith, a trustee of the library, for urging me to accept the invitation when my strong desire had been to forgo the honor in favor of a more qualified speaker, chosen from a dozen or more candidates whose names came easily to mind. I am also grateful to Drake McFeely, president of W. W. Norton, who urged me to expand my lectures and served as my editor, a chore beyond the call of duty and one whose rigors I know all too well. Further thanks to Mr. McFeely for putting me in the hands of his able colleague Sarah Stewart, and his assistant, Eve Lazovitz. Robert Silvers and Barbara Epstein of the *New York Review of Books*, where the first chapter of this book appeared, were, as always, brilliant tutors. My fellow Columbian and erstwhile publishing colleague Robert Gottlieb, the most gifted editor of books of his, and perhaps any, generation, was kind enough to read the manuscript and spared me many errors and omissions. I am grateful to Michael Kazmarek for checking facts, to Alfred Knopf, Jr., and Ashbel Green for their good advice, and to Mary Bahr, Hilton Als, and Veronica Windholtz for their friendship, enthusiasm, and common sense. For further information about Parson Weems, I thank Mr. Hugh Rawson. I must also thank Michael Smolens, my intrepid friend and his fellow visionaries at Three Billion Books for introducing me to the nascent technologies, some still in their garages, that will, in time, realize their vision and mine of the publishing future. For her patience, courage, and wisdom I am, as ever, grateful to my astonishing wife, Judith Miller.

BOOK
BUSINESS

CHAPTER ONE

The Rattle of Pebbles

Trade book publishing is by nature a cottage industry, decentralized, improvisational, personal; best performed by small groups of like-minded people, devoted to their craft, jealous of their autonomy, sensitive to the needs of writers and to the diverse interests of readers. If money were their primary goal, these people would probably have chosen other careers. They might, for example, have become literary agents, many of whom have prospered as authors' royalty guarantees have risen sharply in today's highly competitive market for salable talent. But most publishers and editors I have known prefer to think of themselves as I do, as devotees of a craft whose reward is the work itself and not its cash value.

Today the book business stands at the edge of a vast transformation, one that promises much opportunity for innovation: much trial, much error, much improvement. Long before another half century passes, the industry as I have known it for the past fifty years will have been altered almost beyond recognition. In the 1920s a brilliant generation of young American publishers fell heir to the cultural transformation that became known as modernism and nurtured it with taste, energy, and passion. As Einstein's generation had introduced once and for all the themes of modern physics and as Cézanne, Picasso, and their contemporaries had done the same for painting, the writers of the early twentieth century had created once and for all the vocabulary and themes of modern literature. Much elaboration would follow, but the fundamental work had been done and could not be done again. My career in publishing has traced the long, downward, but by no means barren slope from that Parnassian moment.

The cultural efflorescence of the 1920s was an act of liberation—or so it seemed at the time to its makers—from a society whose moral, aesthetic, and intellectual failings had become intolerable. The transformation that awaits writers and publishers today is much different and will have far greater consequences. It arises not from cultural despair and aesthetic rebellion but from new technologies whose cultural influence promises to be no less revolutionary than the introduction of movable type, a vector of civilization which these new technologies, after half a millennium, have unceremoniously replaced in the last dozen years. As the implications of Gutenberg's technology could not have been foreseen in its own time, those of our own new technologies are indistinct today, but they promise to be no less eventful.

Twenty years ago when my children and their friends came of age I advised them to shun the publishing business, which seemed to me then in a state of terminal decrepitude if not extinction. Today I would offer young people to whom books are precious the opposite advice. The transformation that awaits them foreshadows cultural ramifications that promise a lifetime of creative adventure far more consequential in its much different way than what awaited the generation of Horace Liveright, Alfred Knopf, and Bennett Cerf eighty years ago when

Joyce and Hemingway and Eliot and their peers emerged from the muck of the World War and the terrible innocence that spawned it.

In this book, I want to describe the early stages of these technologies as I understand them. But I cannot do so without discussing the increasingly distressed industry in which I have worked for the past half century. During this time book publishing has deviated from its true nature by assuming, under duress from unfavorable market conditions and the misconceptions of remote managers, the posture of a conventional business. This has led to many difficulties, for book publishing is not a conventional business. It more closely resembles a vocation or an amateur sport in which the primary goal is the activity itself rather than its financial outcome. For owners and editors willing to work for the joy of the task, book publishing in my time has been immensely rewarding. For investors looking for conventional returns, it has been disappointing.

Random House when I joined it in 1958 was a leading American publisher of general-interest books, but its internal telephone directory, listing its hundred or so employees, didn't fill a sheet the size of a postal card. For us in those days Random House was an unusually happy, second family whose

daytime home fit comfortably within the north wing
of the old Villard mansion at Madison and 50th
Street with its black-and-white-marble lobby, its
unreliable elevator, and its courtyard, where we
were entitled to six precious parking spaces: the
other twelve belonged to the Archdiocese of New
York, which occupied the mansion's central and
southern sections. My office, with dark green walls,
worn parquet floors, and a Juliet balcony overlook-
ing the courtyard, had been a bedroom, and from
time to time I came to work and found a wayward
author who had spent the night there, not always
alone. These offices were a second home for authors as well as for ourselves. Mrs. Debanzie, our
Scottish receptionist, usually sent them upstairs to
see us unannounced: W. H. Auden in torn overcoat
and carpet slippers delivering the manuscript of *The
Dyer's Hand*; Ted Geisel, known as Dr. Seuss, arriving
with his storyboards to recite *Green Eggs and Ham* to us
in Bennett Cerf's large, square office at the end of
the hall; Cardinal Spellman submitting his poetry,
which we published as a neighborly act and to fore-
stall controversy with the monsignors over our
parking spaces. In my memory I associate our authors with particular parts of the building: Terry
Southern sitting on a wooden table in the basement

mailroom next to the postage machine, cackling in his exaggerated Texas drawl over scenes he was writing for *Dr. Strangelove*; Andy Warhol outside my office at the head of the once grand but now battered marble staircase, bowing slightly and addressing me in a deferential whisper as Mr. Epstein, as if I were a patriarch and not someone in a torn sweater and corduroy trousers hardly older than he was; John O'Hara in a three-piece suit showing off his Rolls-Royce in the courtyard on a sunny day; Ralph Ellison in my office, smoking a cigar and explaining with his hands how Thelonious Monk developed his chords.

Though our authors relied upon their agents to negotiate their contracts with us, for many of them Random House was their family as much as it was ours. Today most publishing imprints have dissolved within their vast media conglomerates, and many authors now depend on their agents as they once did upon their publishers for general sustenance. But forty years ago, agents were mere peripheral necessities, like dentists, consulted as needed, not the dominant figures in the lives of authors that many of them have since become. In the Villard mansion, editors almost never held meetings but exchanged news and gossip or asked for advice when we felt like it, often from authors who happened to be in the building. In many cases, these authors became our lifelong friends. But at Random House, unlike Simon & Schuster, a much more intimate family in those days, the editors' private lives seldom intersected and we rarely met outside the office. Most of our friendships were with our authors and we jealously reserved these valuable intimacies for ourselves. A regular army lives in a barracks. Guerrilla armies live amid the people who sustain them and for whom they struggle. So do book publishers.

Today the central section of the Villard mansion is the entrance to the Palace Hotel. The southern wing houses a fashionable restaurant. From its entrance you can look up and see my former balcony. By 1969, Random House had acquired Alfred A. Knopf, had been acquired in turn by RCA, and had outgrown the mansion. That spring we moved into a nondescript glass building on Third Avenue. I recall the day joylessly. We were losing more than our parking spaces. We were losing our individuality, I felt, and gaining nothing in return. Though I have been responsible for several innovations in the publishing business, I see now that each of them was intended to recapture the fleeting past. I am skeptical of progress. My instincts are archaeological. I favor the god Janus, who faces backward and forward at once. Without a vivid link to the past, the present is chaos and the future unreadable. In our culture books form such a link, perhaps the main link, certainly an indispensable one. How, I wondered, would the delicate process by which an author's work becomes a book be affected by our new situation? It was with such thoughts that I joined the migration to our new home three blocks to the east. In these new quarters with their carpeted offices we still operated independently of RCA, at least in theory, but a cottage industry within an industrial conglomerate makes no sense. The dissonance between the pretense that we were now an ordinary business and the true nature of our work made me fretful. Only in retrospect did I see that that our removal was part of a much larger transformation, affecting far more than the book publishing business and our small, elegant, amiable firm.

In the 1950s book publishing was still the small-scale, highly personal industry it had been since the 1920s when a remarkable generation of young men, and a few women, many of them Jews who were not welcome in the old-line houses, broke with their genteel predecessors and risked their personal fortunes and the disapproval of their elders by aggressively promoting the literature and ideas of modernism. Like the Manhattan gallery owners of the 1960s, they came of age during a cultural revolution and brilliantly exploited it. But when I encountered them in the 1950s these publishers seemed to me anything but revolutionary. Like the avant-garde writers they championed in the twenties, they were now an establishment and carried their years with dignity. I remember them in tweed caps, wrapped in blankets on the first-class decks of ocean liners; or strolling along Fifth Avenue on Sunday mornings in their topcoats and hats from Locke; or in Hunterdon County in autumn with Faulkner down for the weekend. They lunched at "21" and dined at Chambord and the Colony. After a Sunday lunch at the Knopfs' in Purchase, the shades were drawn and home movies shown of Alfred and Thomas Mann in lawn chairs beside Lake Constance, flickering like automata as they moved their arms in conversation. We stayed for a second silent film showing Mann lecturing, presumably on the moral collapse of German romanticism, for he had drawn a vertical line on a blackboard and on one side had written *beauty, disease, genius,* and *death* and on the other *life* and *morality*. Alfred Knopf might wear dark shirts, sunburst ties, and a Cossack mustache, but he, even more than his staid counterparts, represented the sobriety, the unassailable dignity of his mighty generation in middle age. Their presence was an inspiration to newcomers like myself. To topple them as they had toppled their own predecessors was unthinkable. They were to be emulated. But how? *Ulysses* and *The Waste Land* were not experiments to be perfected by later generations. They were monuments, to be studied but never surpassed. So we and our writers did our best with what we had. Yeats's brave reply to Matthew Arnold's valetudinarian "Dover Beach" lodged in my mind in those days: "Though the great song return no more / There's keen delight in what we have: / The rattle of pebbles on the shore / Under the receding wave."

Soon Random House will move from Third Avenue to a new corporate headquarters to be erected on Broadway by its current owner, an international media conglomerate, which embraces several well-known publishing imprints including, in addition to Random House and Knopf, Doubleday, Bantam, Pantheon, Dell, Crown, and Ballantine as well as a number of British and German imprints. General book publishing in the United States is currently dominated by five empires. Two are based in Germany—Bertelsmann, which owns the Random House group, and Holtzbrinck, which owns St. Martin's and Farrar, Straus & Giroux. Longmans, Pearson, based in London, owns the Viking, Penguin, Putnam, Dutton group, and Rupert Murdoch's News Corporation owns HarperCollins and William Morrow. Simon & Schuster and Pocket Books belong to Viacom, which owns Paramount Pictures and MTV among other media properties. By liquidating redundant overheads these corporate owners hope to improve the low profit margins typical of the industry. But this strategy may be wrong. Because publishers now face severe structural problems arising from an overconcentrated retail marketplace, the new owners may find the business less profitable than ever. Moreover, technological innovations certain to revolutionize the industry will soon render many of the traditional publishing functions of the conglomerates themselves redundant.

Today the telephone directory of the Random House group measures eight-and-a-half by eleven inches, occupies 116 pages, and includes the names of more than 4,500 employees, nearly all of them, I assume, unknown to one another. Nevertheless, the essential tasks at Random House and other publishers are still performed as they always have been, by individual editors and publicists working in small groups with a few writers at a time, though the conditions under which this work is now done differ greatly from those at the old Villard mansion. Conglomerate budgets require efficiencies and create structures that are incompatible with the notorious vagaries of literary production, work whose outcome can only be intuited. How, for instance, does a corporation budget for Norman Mailer's next novel or determine the cash value of such writers as William Faulkner and Cormac McCarthy, whose novels languished for years before they became valuable assets on the Random House backlist? Meanwhile, the retail market for books is now dominated by a few large bookstore chains whose high operating costs demand high rates of turnover and therefore a constant supply of bestsellers, an impossible goal but one to which publishers have become perforce committed. The dissonance I felt when we moved to Third Avenue was premonitory. Our industry was becoming alienated from its natural diversity by an increasingly homogeneous suburban marketplace, demanding ever more uniform products. Books are written everywhere but they have always needed the complex cultures of great cities in which to reverberate. My publishing years coincided with the great postwar dispersal of city populations and the attrition therefore of city bookstores as suburban malls increasingly became the centers of commerce, so that even the well-stocked chain bookstore branches located in cities evoke the undifferentiated atmosphere of shopping malls rather than the cosmopolitanism of the cities to which they happen to have been transplanted.

Many valuable books—most, in fact—are not meant to be best-sellers, and these tend to be slighted in the triage of contemporary publishing and bookselling. I don't mean that fewer books of this sort are being published. Many publishers and their staffs, including the Random House editors today, are still as determined as we were in our old building to find and promote unconventional titles of permanent or even passing value, a commitment manifest in the excellent books chosen by the major review media for their year-end lists. It is my impression that more such books are being published than ever before and more people are reading them, thanks in part to the chains and the online booksellers who have helped make book buying a stimulating part of everyday life. But the life expectancy of many valuable books has declined as chain store retailers are forced to seek ever higher rates of turnover, and morale in the industry suffers accordingly. When this phenomenon first became apparent some thirty years ago, the industry joke was that the shelf life of a book had fallen somewhere between that of milk and yogurt. Since then the situation has worsened and the joke is no longer heard.

In the spring of 1999, Random House published a monumental life of J. P. Morgan,* on which the distinguished biographer Jean Strouse had worked for nearly fourteen years. Her plan had been to finish in four or five years, but Morgan was a surprisingly elusive subject and Strouse is a meticulous scholar. Reviewers called *Morgan* a major contribution to American economic and social history and a vivid portrait of the shy, cyclonic, misunderstood figure who created the modern financial system. Though *Morgan* will interest historians,

---

* I was the editor.

bankers, and economists as well as art historians and collectors, there is nothing recondite about Strouse's book, which appeared on several best-seller lists.

The *Los Angeles Times*, in its year-end list of the best books of 1999, called *Morgan* "a riveting detective story and a masterpiece." *Morgan* was shortlisted by *The New York Times Book Review*, *The New Yorker*, *Time*, *Business Week*, and other general-interest publications as one of the best works of nonfiction of 1999. But when these lists appeared nine months after *Morgan* was published, fewer than a thousand copies were on hand in the 530 superstores of the Barnes & Noble chain, which, together with Borders, the second-largest chain, dominates the retail book trade. With Christmas a month away, Barnes & Noble had apparently decided that in a year when millions of Americans were obsessed with the stock market *Morgan* was nevertheless an unlikely Christmas gift. On the day the *New York Times* list appeared, copies of *Morgan* were no longer on display in Barnes & Noble's branch four blocks north of the Random House building on Third Avenue. It was Strouse's literary agent who visited the Third Avenue store that day, noticed the omission, and called it to the attention of the store manager, who ordered fifty copies. Thereafter, the chains as a whole restocked *Morgan.*

Meanwhile Strouse's book was selling briskly in the independent stores, whose clerks knew their customers' interests and understood *Morgan*'s appeal. But the book chains, offering steep discounts on popular titles, have driven hundreds of independent stores out of business, a process accelerated by Internet retailers, so that fewer than seventy-five major independents employing sophisticated sales staffs and stocking 100,000 or more titles survive. *Morgan* and some of the other "best books" of the year will withstand the bloody triage that is now commonplace in the publishing industry, but many hundreds, even thousands, of other worthy new titles will have vanished by the time next year's best books are chosen. In 1999 some ninety thousand books—many worthless, many others valuable—went out of print, according to the rueful vice-chairman of Barnes & Noble, who is himself constrained by market conditions over which he has no control.

Traditionally, Random House and other publishers cultivated their backlists as their major asset, choosing titles for their permanent value as much as for their immediate appeal, so that even firms grown somnolent with age and neglect tottered along for years on their backlist earnings long after their effective lives were over. But even the strongest publishers depended on their backlists and regarded best-sellers as lucky accidents. In his memoirs, Bennett Cerf, the cofounder and president of Random House, wrote that when Random House acquired the firm of Alfred A. Knopf in 1960 the combined companies could shut down "for the next twenty years or so and make more money than we're making now, because our backlist is like . . . picking up gold from the sidewalk." This incomparable backlist included Kafka, Proust, Camus, Faulkner, O'Neill, Dr. Seuss, James Michener, Wallace Stevens, Ralph Ellison, Thomas Mann, W. H. Auden, and many others, as well as the distinguished Knopf list of cookery books and American historians and the Random House children's list and dictionaries.

When we worked in the Villard mansion, stumbling upon a best-seller was like winning a lottery. In 1959 when *Act One,* Moss Hart's memoir of his life in the theater, appeared on the best-seller list of *The New York Times* we celebrated by closing the office and taking the day off. But it was like having inherited an annuity to publish James Michener and

John O'Hara, who produced best-sellers with reg-
ularity. Every major house could count on three or
four popular writers like these to produce best-
sellers consistently. But the solid foundation—the
accumulated capital—that publishers relied on was
their backlists of books that sold year after year. It
was these books that proclaimed a firm's financial
strength and its cultural standing: a source of pride
which more than compensated the owners and their
staffs for the marginal profits and low wages typical
of the industry.

For authors, it was an honor to join the glitter-
ing backlists of houses like Random House, Knopf,
or Viking or smaller firms of equal distinction,
such as Farrar, Straus & Giroux and W. W. Norton.
But this too has now changed as most publishing
houses have become indistinct in their conglomerate settings. Though some authors remain loyal to
their editors whose advice they find helpful, most
now rely upon their agents to sell their books at
auction. For many of these agents, the only signifi-
cant difference among publishers is how much they
will pay for popular writers or for books of topical
interest that chain-store customers are likely to buy
on impulse or because they have seen their authors
on television. The advantage to authors is obvious,

but many writers, especially promising beginners, are likely to suffer in the long run when their sales fall short of expectations and publishers become wary of their future projects. Today if an author spent the night on my office couch he would be evicted by the security staff. Authors no longer arrive unannounced. They are screened by the guards in the lobby and given name tags to wear on their lapels.

Such name-brand best-selling authors as Tom Clancy, Michael Crichton, Stephen King, Dean Koontz, and John Grisham, whose faithful readers are addicted to their formulaic melodramas, no more need publishers to edit and publicize their books than Nabisco needs Julia Child to improve and publicize Oreos. Name-brand authors need publishers only to print and advertise their books and distribute them to the chains and other mass outlets, routine tasks that all publishers manage equally well and which can be performed as efficiently by independent contractors available for hire: production consultants, publicity agencies, and distribution services. When today's conglomerates learn, as their predecessors did, that book publishing is a high-risk, low-margin business and new investors cannot be found to take their place—when, in other words, publishers cease to exist in their present form—name-brand writers with the help of their agents or business managers may become their own publishers, keeping the entire proceeds from the sale of their books, net of production, advertising, and distribution costs. To retain these powerful authors publishers already forgo much of their normal profit, or incur severe losses, by paying royalty guarantees far greater than can be recouped from sales. As a result, publishers' profits from books by these authors, if there are any after the unearned portion of the guarantee has been deducted from revenues, often amount to little more than a modest fee for services. Given the negligible value that publishers add to these assured best-sellers in today's brand-driven marketplace, these fees are a fair reward.

In effect, name-brand authors are already their own publishers, while their nominal publishers are a vestigial, nonessential convenience, beneficiaries (or victims) of inertia on the part of agents reluctant to forgo the security of a publisher's guarantee. When the conglomerates tire, as they eventually must, of overpaying these star performers, their agents may choose either to produce their clients' books themselves or risk losing their golden eggs to business managers who will do the job for them. In the summer of 2000, Tom Clancy left the agent who had represented him for fifteen years and hired a business manager, Michael Ovitz. He explained that his agent had disappointed him in dealing with Hollywood on his behalf. Ovitz has arranged with other clients to produce their own films and may now do the same for Clancy. He may also arrange for Clancy to become his own publisher, contracting with his existing publisher for production and distribution services. According to *The New York Times* several name-brand film stars, including Leonardo DiCaprio, Kevin Costner, and Robin Williams, have also left their agents recently and hired business managers to create their own production companies rather than sign with studios or independent producers on traditional terms. To prevent conflicts of interest the Screen Actors Guild has denied agents the right to perform this function for their clients, a prohibition confirmed by California law. But under pressure from agents fearful of losing their clients, the guild has considered abandoning this position so that agents too may become their clients' producers. Film stars must nevertheless hire studios to provide technical services, including distribution, for their own productions and for this reason few actors are likely to become their own producers. But the business managers of name-brand writers like Clancy need only contract with production and distribution services to publish their clients' books, or make use of new technologies to offer their books electronically.

It is not only the few predictable best-selling authors who may eventually find that they no longer need publishers. So far the publishing conglomerates have permitted their various imprints to bid against one another to acquire desirable authors, but they may eventually abandon this extravagant concession to the illusion of independence whose *reductio ad absurdum* would be to permit editors within a single imprint to compete with one another in the same way. When the conglomerates end this irrational practice, enterprising agents, no longer able to extract excessive sums for their clients at auction, may be tempted to create Web sites, with the help of editors and publicists, from which their clients' work can be sold directly to readers in printed or electronic form.

Meanwhile, several publishers have begun digitizing their backlists, and Time/Warner, Random House, and Simon & Schuster have launched ex-

perimental projects to publish original manuscripts in digital form for online distribution,
offering traditional royalties. But online distribution of digitized texts sold to consumers on demand requires no investment by publishers in
production, inventory, storage, and many of the
other expenses incurred in conventional book
publishing. The cost of digitizing a text is a few
hundred dollars compared to the many thousands
required to manufacture and distribute physical
books. Moreover, pro-rated Web-site costs per
copy are negligible, so the publisher's actual investment in digital publication consists merely of
allocated editorial, publicity, and general overhead expense. Agents will therefore bargain aggressively for a division of proceeds that reflects
the proportionately far greater value contributed
by the author than the publisher to the digital
process. For their more popular authors, agents
offer their clients' work directly over independent
Web sites, bypassing publishers entirely. Robert
Gottlieb of the powerful William Morris Agency
anticipated the reaction of his fellow agents when
he declared in *The New York Times* in July 2000 that
authors will resist conventional royalties for their
work in digitized form. "These publishers are try-

ing to divide up the new digital world before we have even mapped it out. . . . There is a tremendous reduction in overhead from printing, distribution and all of that, and authors aren't enjoying the benefits of the increased profitability."

For publishers the outcome of this forthcoming struggle over the division of digital income not only will affect new digital publications but will probably force publishers to pay comparable rates for their digitized backlists as well. Some literary agencies with their rosters of loyal clients may therefore become what Random House once was when our authors made themselves at home in the Villard mansion. Who will then represent authors in negotiations with their former agents is an interesting question but not a worrisome one. Old dogs, however, are not good learners. Though Stephen King's enterprising agent in the spring of 2000 contracted with Simon & Schuster to sell King's new book in electronic form on King's own Web site, it seems more likely that independent entrepreneurs in competition with existing publishers, rather than agents, will create literary Web sites for this purpose.

Since an author retains all rights not granted to

the publisher, electronic rights for books published before the mid-nineties, when electronic
publication became an issue, do not belong to
publishers. But book contracts also provide that
authors may not publish versions of their work in
competition with their publishers. This means that
neither authors nor publishers may sell electronic
editions of the majority of backlist titles until the
parties reach a new agreement. In negotiating such
an agreement authors and agents hold the stronger
hand, reflecting not only the greater proportionate value of their contribution to the electronic
product but also the relative strength of their bar-
gaining position. Publishers cannot afford ethi-
cally or financially to withhold the large part of
their backlists from electronic distribution, but
most authors can afford to wait their publishers
out while their agents negotiate for them as a
group. Most likely, the eventual division of electronic backlist proceeds will reflect the terms for
new titles published electronically, and this division will reflect, in turn, not only the greater relative value contributed by the authors but also
competitive pressures on traditional publishers to
match the terms offered by independent authors'

Web sites. One effect of this outcome will be to reduce the value to publishers of their backlists.

Until the new technologies on which this future
depends are widely available in usable form, publishers who once patiently nurtured their authors'
careers as part of their literary capital will remain
short-term gamblers, betting, often rashly, on titles they hope will prove faddish for a season or two,
often without regard to their intrinsic worth or
long-term prospects. This demoralizing inversion
of values has not been a matter of choice on the
part of book publishers but the result of a profound
cultural transformation with roots in the postwar
suburban migration and the homogenized marketplace that resulted, a transformation underway
thirty years ago when Random House migrated
three blocks to the east to its new quarters on Third
Avenue. The dominance of bookstore chains dependent on a regular supply of best-sellers and the
consequent devolution of once proud publishing
houses into units of impersonal corporations is not
the work of thoughtless people or malign forces,
and certainly not of the falsely alleged defects of
suburban culture, but of morally neutral market
conditions—especially the high occupancy costs of

mall premises—that demand rapid turnover of un-differentiated products, rates of turnover that are incompatible with the long, slow, and often erratic lives of important books.

Now the great postwar transformation from city to suburb that created these conditions has, after a half century, begun to play itself out, or as Marxists might say, has become the victim of internal con-tradictions created by emerging technologies in conflict with older forms of production. The old technologies of internal combustion and mass marketing that created the homogeneous suburban marketplace and its chain bookstores are being challenged by technologies that foreshadow a highly decentralized marketplace offering the possibility of nearly infinite choice to buyers at innumerable remote locations. As Marxists might also say, these new forms of production are likely to create new economic relationships, for example by providing greater intimacy between writers and readers, who will no longer depend upon publishers or tradi-tional booksellers to bring them together. The fu-ture of these technologies for book publishing can hardly be foreseen in detail, but their general effect will be to give readers and writers far more direct access to one another than in the recent past and to challenge publishers to acknowledge their reduced role and adapt accordingly.

These new technologies will also test the human capacity to distinguish value from a wilderness of choice, but humanity has always faced this dilemma and solved it well enough over time. The World Wide Web offers access to any would-be writer who may or may not have something to say and know how to say it. Several literary Web sites that have so far emerged are in effect vanity presses or job printers, willing to publish anything, regardless of quality, often at the author's expense. It is highly improbable that from this clutter works of value will emerge. But proven talent will coalesce in particular venues as it always has. Distinguished Web sites, like good bookstores, will attract readers accordingly. The filter that distinguishes value is a function of human nature, not of particular technologies.

An example of these new technologies is machinery that can scan, digitize, and store permanently virtually any text ever created so that other machines can retrieve this content and reproduce copies on demand instantly anywhere in the world, either in electronic form, downloaded for a fee onto a so-called e-book or similar device, or printed and bound for a few dollars a copy, indistinguishable in appearance from conventionally manufactured paperbacks. Machines capable of printing and binding small quantities of digitized texts on demand are already deployed by Ingram, the leading American book wholesaler, by Barnes & Noble and other retailers, and in publishers' warehouses, but future, less expensive versions that are now being developed can be housed in public libraries, in schools and universities, and perhaps even in post offices and other convenient places—Kinko's and Staples, for example: in effect, ATM machines for books. Machines that can print and bind single copies of texts will eventually be common household items, like fax machines today. The advantage to readers in diverse locations who need only supply their credit cards and the appropriate serial numbers to order any text ever written is evident. Readers in Ulan Bator, Samoa, and Nome will have the same access to books as readers in Berkeley and Cambridge. No book need ever go out of print, and readers in search of a particular book, or even specific parts of a book or parts of several books assembled to order, will no longer be frustrated by the mandated turnover requirements of bookstore chains. Though books manufactured one at a time by these machines will cost more to produce than factory-made books, their ultimate cost to readers will be less, since publishers' distribution costs and retail markups will not figure in their price. The convenience of these machines in thousands of locations and eventually perhaps in homes and offices, with access to potentially limitless virtual inventories, catalogued, responsibly annotated, and searchable electronically, will profoundly affect current book-marketing practice, to say nothing of the effect on readers and writers.

In the winter of 2000, Scribners, a division of Simon & Schuster, in a joint venture with Stephen King's own publishing company, Philtrum Press, offered for sale exclusively over the Internet for a limited time at $2.50 per copy King's new 16,000-word ghost story *Riding the Bullet*, which readers could download to their hand-held readers or directly to their screens by means of various software programs. By the end of its first day on sale, 400,000 requests had been received for King's story. Though only 10,000 hand-held reading devices were in use at the time, the technology which gives authors unmediated access to readers is already on the horizon. The rest is up to authors, their agents or business managers, and their publishers.

Far more profound than their impact on writers, readers, and publishers will be the effect of these and other new technologies on the culture itself. Dante's decision seven hundred years ago to write his great poem not in Latin but in what he called the vulgar eloquence—Italian, the language of the people—and the innovation in the following century of printing from movable type are landmarks in the secularization of literacy, and the liberalization of society, as well as an affront to the hegemony of priests and tyrants. The impact of today's emerging technologies promises to be no less revolutionary, perhaps more so. The technology of the printing press enhanced the value of literacy, encouraged widespread learning, and became the *sine qua non* of modern civilization. New technologies will have an even greater effect, narrowing the notorious gap between the educated rich and the unlettered poor and distributing the benefits as well as the hazards of our civilization to everyone on earth. Greater literacy will not reduce the human capacity for mischief any more than Martin Heidegger's philosophical learning kept him from supporting the Nazis, a dilemma that philosophers might explore further. Nonetheless, the spread of learning is good in itself. That these technologies have emerged just as the publishing industry has fallen into terminal decrepitude is providential, one might even say miraculous. For contemporary deists, the timely arrival of the World Wide Web may replace the watch found in the desert as evidence of a divine maker's intricate design.

Until these new technologies become commonplace, easy to use, and capable of reliably encrypting copyright material, publishing conglomerates comprising the ghostly imprints of bygone firms will continue to seek profits by shedding redundant facilities, but they will eventually confront the constraints on profits that publishers have always faced. When they do, they will either contract or collapse under their own weight as their managers discover that a mélange of imprints within a single firm compounds the risks and inefficiencies that are intrinsic to the work. Trade book publishing has always depended on the generosity of patrons and the undercompensated devotion of employees and owners. It has never rewarded investors looking for normal returns, which is why the entertainment conglomerates—CBS, ABC, RCA, MCA-Universal—that acquired such distinguished houses as Henry Holt, G. P. Putnam, and Random House, including Alfred A. Knopf, in the 1970s and 1980s, deluded by the false promise of synergy, eventually found them a burden on their balance sheets and disgorged them. The million-copy sales of a few name-brand best-selling authors led these conglomerates to believe incorrectly that general book publishing is a mass-market business, like selling soap or razor blades or movies. Between 1986 and 1996 the share of all books sold represented by the thirty top best-sellers nearly doubled as retail concentration increased. But within roughly the same period, sixty-three of the one hundred best-selling titles were written by a mere six writers, Tom Clancy, John Grisham, Stephen King, Dean Koontz, Michael Crichton, and Danielle Steel—a much greater concentration than in the past and a mixed blessing to publishers, who sacrifice much of their normal profit, and often incur losses, to keep powerful authors like these. But name-brand best-selling authors may follow King's innovation to its logical next step and exploit their electronic rights without the help of their publishers. Simon & Schuster's press release rejoiced innocently that the electronic distribution of King's new book "bypasses the traditional year-long publishing cycle," but future electronic books by best-selling authors may bypass publishers altogether.*

The atypical sales of these popular writers constitute an entirely different business from the fragmented, idiosyncratic, and unpredictable publication of all other books. Many books in this broader category also become best-sellers, but on a much smaller scale. For these books to sell 100,000 copies is remarkable. Thousands of other titles addressed to specialized interests sell far fewer copies. As an earlier generation of conglomerates discov-

---

* "Citing the popularity of his e-book *Riding the Bullet* . . . best-selling novelist Stephen King plans to release another e-book—this time in installments—and ask readers to pay on the honor system. It also appears he plans to offer the e-book without the help of Simon & Schuster, his old-media publisher, raising new questions about the ability of powerful authors to become powerful new-media self-publishers." *Publishers Weekly*, June 19, 2000. *The New York Times* reported on August 1 that an estimated 152,132 copies of the first installment had been downloaded within a week of its release online.

ered, the excessive royalty guarantees demanded by the authors of predictable best-sellers render their profitability problematic, while the profitability of books in the broader category is made problematic by the unpredictability of their sales. When the conglomerators of the 1970s and 1980s found that instead of acquiring a stable of star performers they had become a source of high-risk capital for the acquisition of future titles by their component publishers, they abandoned the field.

When General Electric, a famously well-run company, acquired RCA in 1986, it immediately expelled two divisions that didn't meet its standard of profitability: a poultry grower and Random House. Twelve years later Advance Publications, the new owner of Random House, came to the same conclusion. The overseas media empires that have since acquired the remains of these publishing firms may soon find that the electronic exploitation of their backlists is their only profitable asset. But these backlists may stagnate should authors follow King's example and sell their future works to their readers directly, as Dickens sold his novels chapter by chapter in his own magazine, *Household Words*, or as Whitman sold his self-published 1855 edition of *Leaves of Grass* or, for that matter, as Shakespeare produced his own plays at the Globe. A generation ago, authors often earned large sums by selling pre-publication rights to their work to mass magazines—*The Saturday Evening Post, Collier's,* and so on—a practice that originated in the nineteenth century when mass-circulation magazines first appeared. Television destroyed this market, but so-called first serial rights may become profitable again when Web site distribution becomes routine and improved technologies provide easy access to the Internet and convenient ways to download electronically distributed literary work.

New technologies will radically change the way books are distributed, but they will not displace the essential work of editing and publicity. Manuscripts are turned into books only by hand, one step at a time. This work may take years as authors with the help of editors construct their manuscripts, so that when the book finally appears—if it does; some never do; the process is fraught with hazards and disappointment—the editor's emotions are almost as much committed to the outcome as the author's. For books of lasting value there is no use hurrying this work for the sake of a schedule or a budget. Profits and orderly procedures, to the extent they can be achieved, are essential to the work, but they are not its purpose any more than breathing is the purpose of life or a scorecard is the purpose of a tennis match. Except for the questionable advantage of computers over typewriters and inkhorns, new technologies will not simplify or enhance this process, which is often as improvisational as writing itself. The decision to accept or reject a manuscript, the strategies of revision and publicity, the choice of artwork and typography when a satisfactory manuscript is finally produced, the emotional and financial support of authors: these can be done only by human beings endowed with the peculiar qualities that make up a successful publisher or editor no matter how the technological environment transforms the rest of the publishing process. Except in rare cases, authors will always need editorial valets to polish their syntax and replenish their purses, share their anguish and their joy, and submerge their own egos for the sake of their authors' fame.

It is less clear how new technologies will transform retail bookselling as the chains in their oversaturated marketplace face competition from Internet booksellers and the prospect of limitless virtual inventories available on demand in electronic or printed form at random locations. These factors have already discouraged investment in the retail chains, whose share prices have stagnated at low levels. Nonetheless, a civilization without retail booksellers is unimaginable. Like shrines and other sacred meeting places, bookstores are essential artifacts of human nature. The feel of a book taken from the shelf and held in the hand is a magical experience, linking writer to reader. But to compete with the World Wide Web, bookstores of the future will be different from the mass-oriented superstores that now dominate the retail marketplace. Tomorrow's stores will have to be what the Web cannot be: tangible, intimate, and local; communal shrines, perhaps with coffee bars offering pleasure and wisdom in the company of others who share one's interests, where the book one wants can always be found and surprises and temptations spring from every shelf.

CHAPTER TWO

Young Man from the Provinces

Random House when I joined it in 1958 was entirely different from Doubleday, my first employer, where I had spent the previous eight years. At Doubleday, the highly profitable book clubs—the Literary Guild was the largest—defined the company's culture, including that of the publishing division. Doubleday was run by direct-mail marketers who knew how to maximize book club margins but knew nothing about how books were actually conceived, gestated, and born. These men were not readers and could not empathize with people who were. For them, books were a commodity—one whose individual peculiarities were an unavoidable inconvenience. They would have been just as happy selling rose bushes or oranges by direct mail. I am grateful to these genial old Doubleday hands for patiently teaching me how to create direct-mail campaigns, which helped when some friends and I launched *The New York Review of Books* in 1963 and when we later owned some book clubs ourselves and later still when I launched the Library of America by direct mail in the mid-1980s, when the independent bookstores on which I had counted to distribute the series had begun to disappear. Doubleday's mail-order executives, red-faced portly men of the old school in blue suits and polished shoes, were decent people, eager to share their wisdom with novices like me, but they were not obsessed by books and did not share my sense of their vital importance. At Doubleday's book clubs, the monthly selections whizzed by the million along a production line and out the door while through another door the memberships poured in, in response to mailings calibrated to succeed if two people in a hundred responded to the offer of free books as inducements to join. It was with similar efficiency that Doubleday's management expected the publishing operation to function. In this sense Doubleday anticipated the constraints of today's overrationalized industry. Such efficiency was, of course, impossible. Clara Claussen, the outspoken Doubleday cookbook editor, who befriended me during my first weeks on the job, warned that the company I had just joined was so badly run that if it were not making so much money it would go out of business tomorrow. Despite her ellipsis I would soon discover that she was right. Without the book club profits Doubleday's publishing operations, geared to the production of best-sellers, would not have survived.*

The book clubs were paying the bills and calling the wrong tunes. Doubleday's publishing division was therefore devoted to commercial ephemera aimed at unsophisticated readers, while its backlist deteriorated and its more literary editors complained of being trapped, like Chaplin, in the gears of a machine that went nowhere and produced nothing. This had not always been so. Under its

---

*A former Doubleday colleague has recently told me that the company treasurer at this time advised the owner that she would be better off selling the company and investing the proceeds in government bonds. Her son eventually sold the business and bought a baseball team with the proceeds, a profitable investment.

founder, Doubleday published Kipling, Conrad, Maugham, and many lesser nobility. But under a second generation of family management more interested in the profitable book clubs than in books themselves, Doubleday's list with few exceptions lacked substance. Its editors received the low wages typical of the industry but not the compensating reward of pride in their work.

As a beginner, I was placed in a cubicle with walls made of white pegboard, a kidney-shaped desk in what was then the modern style, a telephone, and a typewriter and given each morning a pile of manuscripts to read and reject. Except for my friend Clara's frequent visits to warn me of disasters, I was left alone to learn for myself how the business worked. Officially I was a trainee. The plan was that I would work for a month in the editorial department and then move on to sales and production to see where I best fit in. But it was obvious that the editorial department was the head and the other departments the necessary hindquarters of the business, and I had no doubt where I belonged. At the end of my first month on the job I said that I preferred not to move on. Ken McCormick, Doubleday's chief editor and later a

dear friend with a fine, muted sense of the absurd
which he only imperfectly disguised beneath a
merely superficial interest in protocol, said I could
stay put for a while, and until I quit Doubleday
eight years later I did.

Doubleday's editors had private offices of various sizes according to their rank, free-form modern furniture in vivid colors, and surprisingly few
books on their shelves. Those that they had were
displayed on cardboard easels beside posters that
declared them to be swashbuckling epics and
thrilling masterpieces. The editors did not sit at
their desks reading manuscripts as I had imagined
they would but spent most of their time on the
phone or in meetings. The more literary ones usually returned from lunch late in the afternoon,
drunk. Gradually I introduced myself and was welcomed warmly but for several weeks was given no
further assignment than to read unsolicited manuscripts, which I soon learned could be disposed of
on the evidence of a paragraph or two. The gift of
storytelling is uncommon. It can be seen at a glance
even by a beginner like myself. There are rare exceptions. My friend William Styron when he was a
young manuscript reader for McGraw-Hill found

it tedious to read an account of a trans-Pacific journey from east to west by balsawood raft. The book was *Kon-Tiki*, a huge best-seller and an anthropological classic. Styron tells this story to show that he was meant to be a novelist, not a publisher. But I was meant to be a publisher, grateful to leave the agony of creation to others.

I had stumbled at the age of twenty-two into this job with no idea that I would remain in the publishing business for half a century. My plan was to work for a few months, long enough to pay the rent on an apartment I had just taken in Greenwich Village, and then quit to pursue my literary interests. But my standards were high and I knew that I could not become a writer equal to my expectations. That I might be unable to support myself without a job did not occur to me. In the exuberance of youth I must have assumed that something would turn up. Something did: an entirely unexpected career in publishing which for fifty years I considered temporary. During all this time I kept the walls of my office bare and my desk drawers empty. I was prepared to flee in an instant without a backward glance. It was this illusion of freedom—this belief that I wasn't really there at all—that made it possible for me to spend a lifetime in the business.

In that golden autumn of 1950, New York's air quivered with promise. I was thrilled to enter the Time-Life Building at 14 West 49th Street, where Doubleday had its offices, and to know that I was now part of this glamorous world. I knew nothing about book publishing beyond what I had learned the week before I joined Doubleday from a film called *The Scoundrel*. In this film Noël Coward played a publisher of the 1920s, based on the career of the actual publisher Horace Liveright. The screenplay was written in part by Ben Hecht, a writer well known at the time but since forgotten who had once worked for Liveright and hated him. Liveright, I later learned, had not been a scoundrel at all. He was a brilliantly innovative if suicidal publisher addicted to drink and dangerous love affairs. He was as handsome as Coward himself, with an uncanny eye for talent and the promotional instincts of Barnum at a time when writers of genius were turning up on both sides of the Atlantic but were generally shunned by the genteel publishers of the day. Liveright was the first of the so-called Jewish publishers, who as a group would soon energize the somnolent book trade long dominated by houses rooted in the prejudices of the previous century. In the early 1920s he had the field almost to himself.

He published T. S. Eliot, Ernest Hemingway, Theodore Dreiser, Eugene O'Neill, Hart Crane, E. E. Cummings, and William Faulkner as well as Djuna Barnes, S. J. Perelman, Peter Arno, Dorothy Parker, Mike Gold, Nathanael West, and Sigmund Freud. If not for Joyce's anti-Semitic American adviser, who refused to cooperate, Liveright would have fought the censors over *Ulysses* a decade before Random House took the case to court and won. Liveright's European scout was Ezra Pound, who would later become notorious for his anti-Semitic broadcasts during World War Two, but when he worked for Liveright he defended him from Eliot's complaints about his "Jew" publisher. Eliot had told his friend Wyndham Lewis, a crank who savaged the Bloomsbury writers and later became an admirer of Hitler, not to publish with Liveright, but Pound told Lewis that Liveright "was the only American publisher with enough pride to *want* to bring out a book. The rest are worms, humble worms without enough self-respect to appeal to." Liveright also published the Modern Library, the indispensable source in the interwar years of literary classics, major translations, and important modern writers. By 1925 his extravagance forced him to sell the Modern Library to his young employee Bennett Cerf and his friend Donald Klopfer. This purchase became the platform from which they launched Random House two years later.

The Modern Library included a translation of *The Charterhouse of Parma*, Stendhal's delicious novel about a young man as shrewd and guileless regarding life's possibilities and as unconcerned with its hazards as Liveright himself. Thanks to one of those uncanny juxtapositions that supply the grace notes to one's life, I happened to have bought a used Modern Library copy of *The Charterhouse* in a secondhand bookstore on lower Fifth Avenue, a few steps away from the theater where later that day I saw *The Scoundrel*. Despite Ben Hecht's harrowing portrait of Liveright, *The Scoundrel* convinced me to take the job at Doubleday that I had been offered the week before. Eighteen months later when I launched Doubleday's Anchor Books, the intellectually oriented series of paperbacks that precipitated what to my surprise became known as the paperback revolution and did, in fact, reshape the publishing industry, *The Charterhouse of Parma* was the first title on the list.

Liveright was impulsively generous. His offices in an old brownstone on West 48th Street were famous for the impromptu parties that usually began in late afternoon when the bootleggers made their deliveries and lasted till dawn when the last drunken authors and the chorus girls whom Liveright had been interviewing for the Broadway shows in which he recklessly invested the firm's money staggered home. He was as insouciant in his personal life as he was with the firm's assets, but he was also a brilliant innovator devoted to his writers, whom he promoted as flamboyantly as if they were film stars. He was largely responsible for transforming the staid publishing industry of his day into the exciting business that I discovered when after a few weeks on the job I ventured beyond my Doubleday cubicle and began to see what the larger world of book publishing was like.

I forget how the film finally disposed of Liveright, but in real life he was forced to turn his once glamorous firm over to his bookkeeper, an odious man named Arthur Pell to whom he had been selling his shares in an effort to remain solvent. Pell subsequently made his living peddling reprint rights to the remains of Liveright's glorious backlist. It was from him that I bought the rights to C. K. Scott Moncrieff's translation of *The Charter-*

house of Parma for the first Anchor list.* Occasionally
I would see Pell, a short man with a large head and
coarse features, at the theater, courting aging chorus girls whom he had probably met in the twenties
at Liveright's parties. Liveright had spent a miser-
able year in Hollywood after he left the firm and
returned to New York broke. He had long since lost
his rich wife and his apartment on West 57th Street
and was living in a shabby hotel not far from the
gloomy offices which the firm had taken when the
brownstone was sold to raise cash. Since Liveright
had nothing else to do, he would stop in now and
then at these new offices to visit his former colleagues. One day he was sitting in the reception
room when Pell noticed him. "Horace," he said,
according to Liveright's biographer, Tom Dardis,†
"I don't think you ought to come in anymore. It
doesn't look good for business." Pell, having made
off with Liveright's business, was now trying to assume his identity and didn't want the original available for comparison. A few months later, Liveright

---

* Now supplanted by Richard Howard's brilliant translation for the
  Modern Library.
† I have depended upon *Firebrand*, Dardis's biography of Liveright,
  for much of what I have written here about his subject.

was dead and Ben Hecht, whom Liveright had once supported, sat down to write *The Scoundrel.*

Doubleday's offices were a block north of where Liveright's brownstone once stood. But Doubleday might have been on a different continent for all the resemblance it bore to its erstwhile neighbor. More appropriate to Liveright's spirit and to my own was the apartment that I had found on West Tenth Street in Greenwich Village for $69 a month. It had once been the attic of a large townhouse that a previous tenant in the 1920s had fitted out like a set for *La Bohème.* It had a gabled skylight facing north and casement windows under the eaves with boxes of geraniums overlooking rooftops and chimney pots to the south. On clear days the place was awash with sunlight. The walls were faded red brick with traces of white paint, and the fireplace had a copper hood. A tuba had been made into a lamp that could once have been turned on and off by pressing the valves, but the mechanism no longer worked. It was a good place for large parties, so battered by its previous occupants that further damage hardly mattered.

It was at one of these parties that I first met Wystan Auden and his friend Chester Kallman and became aware of Auden's unsettling habit of arriving an hour or so before the appointed time so that he could be home in bed by nine. His American friends, to whom Auden often lectured on the importance of manners, were patient with his eccentricities, but at Oxford, where he was in residence many years later, his premature arrivals provided his colleagues an excuse not to invite him a second time. He served out his term there in cheerless solitude.

Barbara, my future wife, lived around the corner from Tenth Street at Bank and Hudson, and she and her Harvard friends Frank O'Hara and John Ashbery had invited Auden and Kallman, whom they had recently met in one of their precocious forays into New York's literary world. The party was to begin at six. At four I went out to buy the supplies. When I returned a half hour later, Wystan and Chester were waiting for their drinks while Barbara, who had turned up in the meantime, tried to amuse them. Since no one else arrived until seven, we were well into our second bottle of vodka before the party got underway and Wystan went home to bed.

The thrilling Eighth Street Bookstore, a bibliographer's paradise and an informal school for many fledgling publishers in those days, was then at the corner of Eighth and MacDougal, a ten-minute walk from my new apartment. It was here that the idea for Anchor Books first occurred to me, amid neat shelves lined with hardcover editions of all the works in print of Proust, Kafka, Yeats, Auden, and Eliot, with Kant, Hegel, Marx, and Weber, with Pushkin, Chekhov, Turgenev, Dostoevsky, and Tolstoy, with Melville, Whitman, Dickenson, James, Frost, and Faulkner, with volumes of criticism by I. A. Richards, Edmund Wilson, and John Crowe Ransom among others, and with the works of enough other authors like these to satisfy a bookish lifetime. Even now I recall their titles with the same intensity of feeling as that aroused by old songs: *After Strange Gods*, *The Winding Stair*, *The Eighteenth Brumaire*, *Amerika*, *The Age of Anxiety*, *Scoop*, *First Love*, *Dead Souls*, *Bend Sinister*, *Loving*, *The American Scene*, *The Future of an Illusion*, *A Masque of Reason*, *Practical Criticism*, *The Wound and the Bow*.

I visited Eighth Street nearly every day after work, often for hours at a time, but my Doubleday salary was $45 a week and these books were more than I could afford. When I suggested to Ted and Eli Wilentz, the brothers who owned the store, that paperback editions of their books might sell well to people like me, they agreed, and with their encour-

agement I began to look into the possibility of publishing such a series. In those days most paperbacks
were cheaply made reprints of popular novels distributed by magazine wholesalers mainly to newsstands along with the monthly shipments of
magazines, and removed at month's end to make
way for new titles. What I had in mind were sturdier
paperback editions of books of permanent value,
like those displayed by the Wilentz brothers.* They
would be printed on much better paper than drug-

---

* Paperback books were, of course, nothing new. Sermons, cate-
chisms, political and household tracts, and so on were published
in America as paperbacks before the nineteenth century. By the
twentieth century E. Haldemann-Julius had begun publishing his
Little Blue Books at five cents each. These tracts introduced immi-
grants to useful skills and American customs. Dover Books,
launched in the 1940s, reprinted a fascinating collection of
mostly public domain titles that had gone out of print. But these
books were not widely distributed and were intended to satisfy
mostly arcane interests.

Anchor Books and other so-called quality paperbacks would
make available to serious readers of limited means a wide range of
active titles that had heretofore been available only in expensive,
hardcover editions. As the *Little Blue Books* introduced generations
of new Americans to the rudiments of American culture, "quality
paperbacks" would introduce generations of college students to
the materials of world culture.

store paperbacks and be stocked permanently in bookstores for readers like me who could not afford the hardcover versions. Penguin had begun to sell its paperbound classics in the United States, and its success helped convince me that a similarly sophisticated series, oriented toward American readers, would probably succeed too. At first I considered starting this business on my own. But after a few months at Doubleday I saw that launching such a project was more than I dared handle. Moreover I calculated that the initial investment would be about $25,000, a vast and inaccessible sum at the time. So I returned to my cubicle while the idea ripened in my mind.

I had installed on the bookshelves of my new apartment, alongside my Oxford editions of the English poets and my Kittredge Shakespeare with its torn binding, a leather-bound set of the collected works of Walter Pater, which I still own. Pater, a passionate but timid aesthete, had been Oscar Wilde's mentor at Oxford. He was famous for having advised his disciples that life's goal was not the fruits of experience but experience itself. Had he written in the 1920s he would have recommended burning the candle at both ends. In the 1960s and 1970s he would have stood on the sidelines of the cultural rebellion and been appalled. Though Pater was too timid to follow his own doctrine and eventually disappointed Wilde, his star pupil, he nevertheless urged his followers to "burn with a hard gemlike flame," which Wilde of course did, and so, I had decided when I read Pater in my teens, would I, once I learned how. I never did.

What combination of genes and infantile misadventures attracted me in my late adolescence to Pater's aestheticism I have no idea, but the potentiality must have existed when I arrived from the provinces and entered Columbia in 1945, an auspicious time in the illustrious history of that great college. The professors were learned, fluent, and worldly and considered the education of undergraduates their main obligation if not their greatest pleasure. In those days literary theory in the form of "the new criticism" flourished at Yale but was disregarded at Columbia where students, with the help of their teachers, were expected to make whatever sense they could of the books they were assigned. The classes were small, the fees were $400 a term, and a few students, including myself, responded to their teachers so avidly that Dante, Shakespeare, Coleridge, and Keats became our obsessions too. We spent our days and nights in Butler

Library reading whatever we could find about these and other writers and formed the habits of a lifetime. Then as now at Columbia, every undergraduate had to read the great literature of the world, which then extended from Athens to London and Dublin with an unexplored province in the eastern United States. I would have been happy to remain forever an undergraduate reading the authors whose manly names encircled the frieze of Butler Library, but a year of graduate school—an employment service for future professors—convinced me that I was not made for academic life. Instead the publishing business became an extension of my undergraduate years, a personal college in which my authors have been my teachers and their works in progress my curriculum. I cannot imagine a happier way to have spent this half century.

When I became a publisher it was my undergraduate encounter with books that I wanted to share with the world. I believed and still do that the democratic ideal is a permanent and inconclusive Socratic seminar in which we all learn from one another. The publisher's job is to supply the necessary readings. But in 1951, publishers were not performing this function well, and Anchor Books seemed to me an obvious corrective.

The freshman class of 1945 included many veterans, some still wearing their flight jackets and Marine Corps tunics, most of them eager to begin their civilian careers. Among these veterans were a few aesthetes who had spent the war years—some had actually been under fire—reciting Dante and Racine at Anzio or translating classical Chinese poetry on a destroyer in the South Pacific. This coterie adopted me as its pupil, and to its five or six members I owe my belief, now much modified but not abandoned, that literature is not a pastime like golf or bridge but a kind of religion whose gods are manifest in the works of great writers. What else, I would ask myself in all seriousness, could have inspired *The Divine Comedy* or *The Tempest* if not a divine spirit? Shakespeare, I have since learned, had no supernatural help, and neither did Dante despite what he himself may have written. Nevertheless the young are drawn to great simplifications, and I was no exception.

Whittaker Chambers, the former Communist who denounced his erstwhile friend Alger Hiss, and Thomas Merton, the Trappist monk who became famous as the author of *The Seven Storey Mountain*, had studied at Columbia in the 1930s, and both Marxism and an intellectualized form of Catholicism were still very much in the air. But Marxism was too worldly for my ethereal tastes and too narrowly apocalyptic to offer a convincing account of human possibility. With its promise of redemption in the indefinite future and in the meantime iron discipline under the self-invented laws of history it differed, to me, only in its décor from Catholicism. Though I much preferred and was intrigued by Catholic décor, conversion required a suspension of disbelief in transparent absurdities of which I was incapable. Moreover, I had been raised in a Catholic town and had heard enough from my terrorized schoolmates about the crime and punishment of carnal affection to know that the sex-besotted, dictatorial Church was not for me. Instead I became a Platonist. To my retrospective horror I argued bitterly one evening with a favorite professor, as we stood in the doorway of Butler Library while the snow swirled around us, that Plutarch was foolish to interest himself in merely human qualities and should have contemplated ideal forms rather than written profiles of actual people.

It is no wonder that Doubleday's personnel manager told me while I filled out some forms during my first week on the job that he didn't see how I could last longer than a week or two in the publish-

ing business. But after a few months at Doubleday I
found that literature, like all religions, is also a
business, though not a very good business. As I ex-
plored the prospects for the paperback series I had
in mind, I introduced myself to Doubleday's production manager, a florid, smiling gentleman of
fifty or so with a wisp of white hair. He owned a collection of colorful tweed jackets and that day wore a
black-and-white houndstooth with side vents in the
British style. The bachelor button on his lapel
matched his eyes. I seem to remember that above
his desk hung a photograph of himself taken at Bel-
mont Park. If my memory is correct he wore the
same jacket and stood beside a garlanded racehorse
in the Winner's Circle.

His name was Harry Downey, and he showed me
how to find the point at which a book breaks even
by subtracting from net revenues received the costs
of paper, printing, binding, royalty, and advertising, together with various overhead allocations, and
dividing the remainder into the cost of composition, plates, artwork, and so on. Thus if the cost
per copy of paper, printing, binding, royalty, and
advertising is $1 and allocated overhead costs for
sales expense, rent, heat, light, and administration
are another $1 and revenue is $3 per copy, then if

the one-time costs of composition and plates—say $3,000—are divided by the remaining dollar, the book can be expected to break even at three thousand copies, provided the royalty guarantee to the author has been earned out by that point. When this hypothetical book has broken even, the $1 per copy that amortized the cost of composition and plates becomes profit on every subsequent sale. This is why Bennett Cerf said that Random House could make more money if it simply lived off its rich backlist than if it continued to speculate on new titles, but it was Harry Downey who first introduced me to the fundamental principle that the function of the front list is to enhance the backlist, a principle that Doubleday, alas, largely ignored and that today's retail chains with their dependence on ephemera have made it difficult for publishers to obey.

The series of so-called quality paperbacks that I was planning would consist of predictably long-lived titles, books that would sell year after to students like me who now numbered in the millions. Therefore, profits accrued from previous lists would support future publications and soon the project would be self-sustaining, unlike Doubleday's hardcover titles, most of which barely survived the season in which they were published, forcing Doubleday to re-create itself almost anew year after year.

In the early 1950s, book publishers and Doubleday in particular were not yet attuned to the postwar generation that had already begun to turn the world of its parents upside down. Since I belonged to this new generation I could see numerous anomalies created by this demographic fault line that were invisible to my elders at Doubleday and other book publishers. The most obvious of these and the one that led to Anchor Books was the unnecessary difficulty placed before readers like myself because the writers we had discovered in college were either out of print or available only in expensive hardcover editions, like those I coveted at the Eighth Street Bookstore. Before the war, college had been a privilege. Now it was a necessity, and thanks to the GI Bill and other federal programs, millions of my contemporaries were enrolled. I didn't think much about politics in those days, but in retrospect it is obvious that the GI Bill was a glorious attempt to fulfill the promise of American democracy, along with the Marshall Plan and later the civil rights legislation of the 1960s, even if the latter two were conceived partly as Cold

War strategies rather than for their own sake. At the time I took such heroic politics for granted. We had just saved the world from two terrible enemies. Why shouldn't we continue to do great and decent things?

The 1950s are conventionally recalled as complacent and conformist, a half-truth propagated by two influential titles in the Anchor series—David Riesman's *The Lonely Crowd* and W. H. Whyte's *The Organization Man*. But these years were also a highly creative, golden age in which the rights and privileges of citizenship would soon be extended well beyond their prewar boundaries if hardly to their ultimate limits. To be sure, Senator McCarthy had introduced the vocabulary of *ad hominem* denunciation over political differences that haunted public discourse during the Cold War, and the United States was already stumbling blindly into a very hot war by supporting the French effort to recolonize Vietnam. But the Korean War had ended in 1953 and the Vietnam mess was not yet visible. In 1953 no politician would dare tell voters that their happiness depended upon places called Laos and the Gulf of Tonkin. The terrors of the Depression were receding. Eisenhower was grinning and golfing, and for those of us made uneasy by this presidential complacency there was the impish Adlai Stevenson to pull Eisenhower's tail harmlessly at election time. McCarthy would soon destroy himself if not his legacy, and the maternity hospitals were bursting with the Baby Boom. A postwar generation of American writers and artists had emerged. Manhattan would soon replace Paris as the world's cultural emporium, and Duke Ellington and Billy Strayhorn were writing its score. On warm summer nights you could hear Tatum and Monk through the open doors of the clubs on West 52nd Street without spending a penny, or if you had a few pennies you could buy a beer at the Vanguard or Café Society and hear Mabel Mercer and Ella Fitzgerald sing the lyrics.

It was a good time to be young in America and magical to be young in New York. It seemed to me inevitable that my new series would succeed, and I was not nearly as surprised as I should have been when Ken McCormick approved the business plan that I drew up with Harry Downey's help. At the time his approval seemed only natural, but it took courage on his part to entrust an eccentric twenty-two-year-old with barely a year's experience with such a project. The New York booksellers whom I visited were as encouraging as the Wilentz brothers had been, especially Arnold Swenson at the Columbia University Bookstore and Lillian Friedman at Brentano's on Fifth Avenue; she eventually turned her entire basement over to Anchor Books and the many competing series that soon followed. The first Anchor list of twelve titles included *To the Finland Station*, Edmund Wilson's study of the intellectual sources of the French and Russian revolutions; D. H. Lawrence's *Studies in Classic American Literature*; novels by André Gide and Joseph Conrad; and, of course, *The Charterhouse of Parma*. The prices ranged from 65 cents to $1.25, and I calculated that each title would break even at about twenty thousand copies. Mass-market paperbacks sold in drugstores and newsstands were printed on inexpensive paper called ground wood that turned brown upon contact with light, and their covers were coated with a kind of cellophane that peeled away with use. I decided to print Anchor titles on a more expensive and durable acid-free sheet that retained its whiteness somewhat longer and to print the covers on heavy stock in a matte finish. The covers were designed by friends who were artists, of whom the most notable was Edward Gorey, another of Barbara's Harvard classmates. He would later become famous for his macabre drawings. The distinctive

format announced the intentions of the series un-
mistakably and had much to do with its success,
though it was the titles themselves that identified
Anchor Books with the spirit of the new age.

The success or failure of the projects I have been
involved with has always been apparent from the earliest vibrations. Timing is essential, as it will certainly
be in the exploitation of the electronic literary marketplace that is just over today's horizon. For Anchor
Books, the timing was perfect. Within a year other
publishers, including Knopf and Random House,
announced quality paperback series of their own,
and soon Lillian Friedman's Fifth Avenue basement
was ablaze with upscale paperbacks. To my dismay, so
was the once staid Eighth Street Bookstore, whose
orderly shelves of hardcovers had so delighted me. By
contrast the racks of quality paperbacks that the
Wilentz brothers had now installed seemed an affront to the store's serene dignity.

I became aware for the first time of my ambiva-
lence toward innovation, even if I happened to be
responsible for it. As my finances improved I found
that I much preferred hardcover editions with their
jackets removed for my own shelves. Though Anchor Books soon became known as the origin of a
paperback revolution, my aim had been to restore

and extend the *ancien régime* of literature, not to make a new world. This has always been my aim.

I was nevertheless surprised to find that I had a flair for innovative work, and I wanted to do more of it. I liked editing manuscripts and working with authors, whom I exploited for purposes of my own education, but I enjoyed even more the mechanics of setting up a business and looked forward to discovering other anomalies to correct. I liked traveling by train from city to city, talking to retail booksellers and wholesalers, and when I was in New York I gossiped with them daily by phone. I was fascinated by production details and budgets and kept track of the orders as they came into Doubleday's mailroom every morning. In those days before the introduction of computerized systems with their abundance of useless and confusing information, publishing houses, even one as large as Doubleday, were small enough so that such intimacy with the work was at once possible, necessary, and a pleasure. As a child I liked math puzzles. Computing the variables of a new business to get an approximate sense of direction provided even greater satisfaction, since the real world was part of the problem.

But I lacked the patience to operate a business day by day. Within a year or so, Anchor Books was well established and very profitable. Since the titles belonged to the postwar intellectual zeitgeist, they all sold well, especially those with Gorey's covers. Moreover the series itself had become a fad and readers were collecting Anchor Books for that reason alone. But I was restless. I had begun to publish the Anchor Bible, a multivolume edition of the Old and New Testaments, book by book, based on archaeological evidence. At the time, publishers were issuing various revisions of the *King James* version, adapted for modern readers. My rather esoteric project had the opposite aim: its editors wanted to distinguish from subsequent interpolations what the biblical authors actually said. The Anchor Bible sold well in the religious market and was soon running smoothly without my help. Future projects, however, I wanted to start on my own, though not for the sake of making money, an activity I regarded then, to my subsequent regret, with Falstaffian disdain. My ambition was evangelical. I wanted to share with the world the literary euphoria I had enjoyed at Columbia College. In those days I thought of myself as a missionary. In fact, I was only a book publisher; however, the vocations differed only in the contents of their respective scriptures.

CHAPTER THREE

Lost Illusions

Despite the success of Anchor Books and my growing affection for my colleagues as I came to know them, I was uneasy at Doubleday. A friend at Columbia had warned me that I would eventually have problems there. As evidence he told me that a half century earlier a young Doubleday editor named Frank Norris, who would soon become an important American novelist—he wrote *McTeague*, *The Pit*, and *The Octopus*, among other works, and died far too young of peritonitis—had come upon the manuscript of a first novel called *Sister Carrie* written by Theodore Dreiser, an obscure Midwestern newspaperman and magazine editor at the time, best known as the younger brother of a famous songwriter. The fate of this manuscript at Doubleday was tragic. On Norris's recommendation the company signed Dreiser to a contract, but when the owner's wife returned at the end of summer from her European holiday and learned that in the novel Carrie, an adulteress, was not punished but instead became a famous actress, she told her husband not to publish the book. Dreiser, cantankerous even at that early age—he would later become much worse— sued rather than find another publisher. Doubleday responded predictably by printing a few hundred copies, most of which it kept in its warehouse, distributing just enough to meet the legal definition of publication. Its eventual sale was 450 copies. Reviews were mixed.

Publishers had good reason to fear censorship in those genteel times, but Doubleday's suppression of Dreiser's great novel was contemptible. The friend who told me this story warned that Doubleday was still a philistine company and would frustrate someone whose illusions about the literary life were as innocent as mine, but I ignored the warning. I was as self-confident as I was naive and felt that if Doubleday disappointed me that would be its misfortune, not mine. Moreover, I assumed that it had learned its lesson and would not make the same mistake again. I would soon discover that I was wrong, a discovery that led to my resignation.

As for Dreiser, Liveright eventually signed him to a generous contract for several books, most of which lost money. Despite these losses and Dreiser's hostile demands for still more money, Liveright, who must have found Dreiser's behavior almost intolerable, was confident that his patience would eventually be rewarded. It was. After much delay, Dreiser submitted the manuscript for *An American Tragedy*, which created a scandal, became a best-seller despite its uncomprehending reviews, and remains an American classic. Then, having quarreled with Liveright—he actually threw a cup of coffee in Liveright's face during lunch at the Ritz, where the two were arguing over the division of income from screen rights to *An American Tragedy*—Dreiser never spoke to Liveright again. Liveright's rise and fall paralleled that of Carrie's tragic lover, George Hurstwood, the glamorous manager of a fashionable Chicago restaurant who let his passion for Carrie get the better of his good sense and died penniless on the Bowery, while Carrie's name blazed forth from the fire signs above the theater in Herald Square where she was starring. I found it odd that Dreiser, who had such sympathy for Hurstwood, should have mistreated his living counterpart who had shown him such generosity, but authors, I would soon learn, sometimes bite when their egos are underfed.

My discovery that Doubleday had not learned its lesson from the Dreiser episode occurred in the following way. When I wrote to Edmund Wilson offering an advance of $900 for permission to include *To the Finland Station* in the first list of Anchor Books, he replied by handwritten postal card accepting my terms and suggesting that I visit him in Wellfleet on Cape Cod. I was delighted to accept and arrived on a Halloween weekend at his green-shuttered house with its sagging porch and wind-scoured shingles that clung to the house like white silk.

I had been given as a graduation present from high school a copy of *Axel's Castle*, Wilson's introduction to the symbolist writers, and had become an admirer of his work, but I did not expect to find that Wilson was also an accomplished magician. On the day of my arrival he had set up in his study a proscenium, and that evening, in the glow of red lightbulbs, he put on a magic show meant to amuse his six-year-old daughter, Helen. However, she quickly tired of her father's strange croaks and glowing skeletons—perhaps she was embarrassed by these antics in the presence of a stranger—and after ten minutes left the room scowling, dragging her embarrassed mother behind her. Thus I was left alone as Wilson gamely went on with the show that he must have been planning for weeks.

That weekend Wilson and I became friends, and thereafter he and his enchanting wife, Elena, and Barbara and I exchanged many visits. At the end of one Thanksgiving weekend several years later as Barbara and I were saying goodbye to the Wilsons, Edmund invited me into his study and handed me a manuscript in two black binders. He told me in his high-pitched, rather breathless voice that the author was his friend Volodya Nabokov, that the novel he had handed me was repulsive and could not be published legally, but that I should read it anyway. Perhaps I would disagree. Moreover, Nabokov did not want his name associated with the manuscript and I must not reveal it to my colleagues if I decided to show it to them.

The manuscript was, of course, *Lolita*. Wilson had recently run afoul of the censors with *Memoirs of Hecate County*, his own rather steamy novel, and his

publisher—Doubleday, it so happened—had to
withdraw the book when the Supreme Court, from
which Justice Felix Frankfurter, a friend of Wilson's, had recused himself, let stand a lower-court
ruling against it. At issue was whether the Constitu-
tion protects a work that includes among other intimate details an account of a woman who puts her
hand on or near a man's private parts. Near might
have been acceptable in the 1940s. On was not.
Wilson's account was ambiguous. The Justices, unable to decide, deadlocked, and Wilson's book was
banned. While the Court pondered this issue, Wilson's novel became a scandalous best-seller. Naturally, Wilson followed the case closely and
considered himself an expert on the Constitutional
niceties being debated. Wilson himself was un-
abashed by descriptions of sexual intercourse. His
published notebooks include many accounts, as
vivid as Melville's descriptions of amorous whales,
of his own rather cetaceous performances. But his
sympathetic interest in the vagaries of human sexu-
ality did not extend to *Lolita*.

I did not find *Lolita* repulsive, nor did I find it
the work of genius that it has since been called. I
admired Nabokov's earlier novels published by New
Directions and preferred their cold precision to

the plummy and it seemed to me rather cruel, if also very funny, *Lolita*, in which Nabokov seemed to be congratulating himself on his jokes. I was puzzled by Nabokov's intentions. *Lolita* seemed to be making a statement. Was Nabokov trying to show that America is unsafe for highly strung émigrés like himself who risk losing their cultural identities to a country as shallow and seductive as his innocently corrupt heroine? Or was he simply elaborating an erotic theme he had touched on in his earlier work? Later, when he and I became friends, I asked him how the idea for *Lolita* had occurred to him. I expected a fanciful answer and was not disappointed. He told me that one day he, his wife, Vera, and his ten-year-old son, Dmitri, had been driving home to Ithaca from a butterfly expedition in the Rockies and stopped for the night in a small Ohio town. Since there was no motel available they took rooms in the home of a Methodist minister. After dinner, when the minister and his wife had retired, Vladimir noticed that Dmitri had disappeared. Vladimir found him under a tree on the lawn in the arms of the minister's teenage daughter. Vladimir told me that this encounter aroused his curiosity about the sexual precocity of teenage American girls, and back in Ithaca would sit behind them on the school bus, notebook in hand, recording their chatter which soon emerged in the pages of his novel. I assumed that this unlikely detail, like the story of the minister's daughter, was Vladimir's way of telling me not to ask foolish questions.

Eventually I would learn how passionately Nabokov wanted to return to his ancestral St. Petersburg once the Communists had been got rid of, which he correctly assumed would eventually happen, though not as soon as he had hoped. This probably explains his determination that Dmitri not be seduced by his American surroundings and why he and Vera never settled down in the United States but lived like cuckoos in the rented houses of Cornell professors on sabbatical leave, ready to fly to his family estates as soon as they were liberated. Perhaps too this is why Vladimir insisted that Pushkin's *Eugene Onegin* (which he liked to call *Gene One Gin*) was impossible to translate into idiomatic English for the same reason that it would be impossible to transpose him and Dmitri into Americans. When the Soviet Union collapsed, Nabokov had been dead for several years. His family mansion in St. Petersburg, I read somewhere, was bought by a twenty-five-year-old instant millionaire, a Nabokovian twist.

Later Nabokov became a defender of the Vietnam War in the mistaken belief that victory over the Viet Cong would hasten the fall of the Soviet Union. Since I disagreed, he interrupted our friendship and dismissed me as the executor of his literary trust. On a Sunday afternoon in August in the early 1970s we met again accidentally in the Paris Ritz, where I had gone to find a cigar and instead found Vladimir seated in a corner of the otherwise deserted bar wearing a loud Hawaiian shirt, pretending to be a boisterous American tourist and addressing in a booming Midwestern voice Vera and another woman, his French translator. We met that evening at the hotel for an early dinner. The Vietnam War had not ended, and Vladimir, still in his Hawaiian shirt, proposed a toast to President Nixon. Vera demurred on my behalf, but I saw no reason, under the circumstances, not to raise my glass. We parted amid expressions of renewed friendship. Despite the flamboyant American style that he had adopted, he was now living in true émigré fashion in Montreaux. I never saw him again.

After I returned from our Thanksgiving weekend at the Wilsons' and read *Lolita*, I passed a note to my Doubleday colleagues acknowledging the legal risks but urging them to publish *Lolita* nevertheless.

I mentioned my literary misgivings but said that the book was obviously a serious performance and should be taken seriously by us. I had quite forgotten the Dreiser affair and my friend's warning. I assumed that Doubleday would be pleased to publish *Lolita.* Meanwhile I visited the Nabokovs in one of their borrowed nests in Ithaca and offered to publish Vladimir's wonderful novel *Pnin,* about an émigré professor at an American university who despite his best efforts cannot adapt to American soil. Vladimir also agreed to let me publish large sections of *Lolita* in *The Anchor Review,* a quarterly magazine that I published as part of the Anchor series. This became *Lolita's* first publication in the United States, and since no legal difficulties arose I saw no reason that Doubleday should not now publish the entire novel.

But Doubleday's president at the time, a lawyer filling in until the next generation of Doubleday children came of age, felt differently. He refused absolutely to read the manuscript and would not under any circumstances discuss it, perhaps because he felt he had exerted himself enough on behalf of the First Amendment in his unsuccessful defense of Wilson's novel before the Supreme Court. He may also have felt that the Doubleday family, which had been horrified a half century previously by *Sister Carrie,* was not yet ready for an amorous night at the Enchanted Hunters.

This president, a man named Douglas Black, was an alarming character. He drank heavily and his moods could not be predicted. At one moment he might burst into song—he was fond of "Some Enchanted Evening" from *South Pacific* and liked to imitate Ezio Pinza's basso performance—and at other moments he would fly into a rage over nothing at all. In either mood he terrorized his employees, one of whom compared him to the loony millionaire in *City Lights* who would give Chaplin the run of his mansion and the next morning order his butler to throw him out into the street. One of my colleagues when he left the president's office one morning delicately brushed imaginary dust from his trousers and paraded jauntily down the corridor swinging an imaginary cane.

For me during these hopeless negotiations over *Lolita* it was as if I had been mistakenly placed in an asylum. If I stayed any longer I would soon be unable to claim that I was there in error. But the *Lolita* mess was not, in itself, the reason for my departure. Anchor Books had now become a very profitable part of Doubleday's publishing operation, proportionately the most profitable part. Fifty years later, it flourishes as part of the Bertelsmann empire. But it was not mine and my commitment to its success had become a trap. The illusion of freedom implied by my bare walls and empty desk was a fraud. Actual freedom meant leaving Anchor Books and starting my own business if I wanted to make my own decisions about what to publish. Money in itself was not the issue, though perhaps it should have been. I now had a family to support, and my Doubleday salary hardly reflected the value of the asset I had created. But this was my fault. To profit from Anchor Books I should have gone into business on my own. It was the *Lolita* mess that convinced me that now was the time to do so. When I left the Doubleday offices for the last time I was—the cliché is unavoidable—walking on air, but my euphoria was nothing compared to Barbara's; to her Doubleday, where she had worked briefly, had always seemed somewhat ridiculous and its excitable president quite mad.

Three days after I quit, I left for London with my friend Barney Rosset, the owner of Grove Press, whose Evergreen paperbacks had become one of Anchor's liveliest competitors. In those days New York's international airport was called Idlewild, after a section of the Borough of Queens. There was a departure lounge but no separate terminals as there are now. Passengers simply walked across the tarmac and boarded their flights. As I climbed the steps to the plane I looked back to wave to Barbara and some friends who had come to see Barney and me off. Barbara was laughing. The others were weeping. They must have thought I had abandoned a brilliant career. In fact I had finally acted upon a decision that I had made eight years previously when I thought I would stay at Doubleday for a month or two and then see what the world had to offer.

Barney was a brilliant and dauntless publisher who would not have hesitated to publish *Lolita* if Nabokov had not in the meantime made other arrangements. He was Liveright's spiritual descendant, the publisher of Beckett, Genet, and Ionesco. If anyone deserves to receive the Curtis Benjamin Award for lifetime achievement in book publishing, he does. He fought the *Chatterley* case and in 1960 won before the Supreme Court, defeating the book censors once and for all. He became the publisher of the Beats. He was also as headstrong, litigious, and impractical as Liveright had been and like Liveright would eventually lose his company.

Despite our much different temperaments we were friends and were on our way to London to buy the American branch of Penguin Books. Had we succeeded, our temperamental differences would have led to trouble and our friendship would have suffered.

A year previously, Alan Lane, the founder of Penguin in the 1930s, had asked me to run his American branch, which consisted then of a distribution center in Baltimore but had no New York office and no American editorial operation. His previous American managers had recently quit to start their own firm, New American Library, which along with Anchor and its many competitors now dominated the American market for upscale paperbacks, leaving Penguin far behind. I refused his offer but said that if he wanted to sell his American operation I could raise the money to buy it. He suggested that we talk further, and as the Nabokov situation worsened we did.

What I didn't grasp at the time was that Lane, like many British publishers, did not own his company; his bankers did. He ran the firm on an overdraft and was, in effect, an employee of his creditors. As our discussions in London progressed, I discovered that Barney and I were not the only American publishers he was talking to. There were at least two others. I surmised what should have occurred to me when he tried to hire me: that he hoped to pay off his bankers by selling his American operation with me as part of the package. Lane was a fine publisher, as sly as he was affable, but his bank was not going to let him escape its clutches by selling off his most promising overseas market to Americans. By midweek it was plain that our plan would come to nothing, a blessing in retrospect, given the slim chance that Barney and I would have gotten along as partners. Years later when Barney's business ran into trouble I helped arrange for Random House to become his distributor. The terms of the deal were generous in my opinion but did not prevent Barney from demanding subsequent improvements. When Random House refused, Barney sued. My admiration for Barney survived, but our friendship was badly dented.

Barney left for Paris to visit Beckett, and I agreed to spend the weekend at Lane's country house, just beyond the runway at Heathrow Airport in Staines, where Lane continued to pretend that he might still be able to make a deal. While I was at Lane's house, Bennett Cerf called to ask how things were going. I said they were not going anywhere, and he replied that he could have saved me the trip. Lane's bankers would no more let him sell his American branch than the Queen would let Prince Philip sell Canada. He suggested that I join him and his partner, Donald Klopfer, at Random House. I could work there as an editor with no additional responsibilities, he told me, and start my own business at the same time. Perhaps he and Donald would invest. Overseas calls were indistinct in those days and the planes taking off from Heathrow made it even harder to hear. But after a week in London I was delighted to hear Bennett's Broadway accent, and we agreed to meet when I got back.

A week later we had a deal. I would bring books to the Random House list and be free to start a company of my own, provided, of course, there was no conflict. It was an unusual arrangement, but Bennett and Donald were unusual men. We were friends. When I think of them now, and I often do, I think of their politeness, their instinctive respect for the feelings of others: a rare form of wisdom. Donald's solicitude was marginally greater. He was naturally graceful. Bennett did not hesitate to interrupt one's solitude when he had a new joke to tell. Only once, I believe, did they fire an editor. They did so reluctantly, but the editor's antics left them no choice. They approached the task with trepidation, but the editor accepted their decision stoically. As he rose to leave he happened to say that he had been intending to buy a house, but now he couldn't. Bennett and Donald lent him the money. When I joined Random House I saw no need for a contract and did not ask for one. Eight years later when Random House belonged to RCA and Bob Bernstein, who had succeeded Bennett as head of the firm, suggested that it was now time for a contract, I asked, "Why? Don't we trust each other?" Bob stared at me. I stared at him and signed the contract. We had not changed but Random House had.

When I worked at Doubleday and lived in Greenwich Village I would sometimes see William Faulkner waiting in the Fourth Street station of the Independent subway line for a train to take him uptown to his Random House editor, Albert Erskine, at the old Villard mansion. Even if I hadn't known who he was, I would have noticed him, a coatless, white-crested, red-faced Mississippi bantam amid the colorless Northern poultry that crowded the rush-hour platform in winter. Under his arm he usually held a package wrapped in brown paper that must in those years have contained galleys of *A Fable* or of *The Town*, part two of the Snopes trilogy he was then completing. What joy, I thought, to be Albert Erskine, working with Faulkner's manuscripts. It was well known that for years Bennett and Donald had supplied Faulkner with money, paid his overdue household bills, pleaded with his Hollywood employers to raise his screenwriter's salary, nursed him through his love affairs, his drunken nights, his hangovers, his falls from the horses he insisted on riding, and tried, not always successfully to keep his books in print when few people wanted them. This act of faith cost both money and time. Bennett and Donald had an aversion to chaos in their own lives and cannot have enjoyed nursing their exotic genius through those drunken nights.

Then in 1946 the literary critic Malcolm Cowley published a collection of Faulkner's writing, which established, at long last, his public reputation, easing Faulkner's financial problems. The Nobel Prize would follow. There were times when Random House had to refuse Faulkner's repeated demands for money, but these rejections were infrequent and sometimes Bennett and Donald reached into their own pockets when they felt the firm had gone far enough. The problem was not Faulkner's extravagance. Until Cowley's imprimatur, his books didn't sell. Despite the efforts of many devoted booksellers to persuade their customers that Faulkner was a native genius, readers were not ready for him. Had Bennett and Donald treated Faulkner as simply an unpromising budget item, he would still have written his novels—the literary will is not so easily thwarted—but Random House might not have been Faulkner's publisher when his audience finally caught up with him.

When Bennett and Donald owned Random House, the last thing they expected to do, as Bennett wrote in his memoirs, was make money, and in this respect they were typical of their brilliant publishing generation. They worked for the joy of the task and to their surprise made an unexpected fortune when they sold 30 percent of the firm to the public in October 1959 and a greater fortune when RCA bought the company for $40 million in January 1966. Though Random House was probably the most successful trade book publisher of its time, it was well known within the firm that the owners took modest salaries, less in several cases than they paid members of the staff, whose incomes they were in effect subsidizing. They were experts at their craft, and among the happiest and surely the sweetest men I have ever known. Traces of their spirit can still be discerned, however faintly, at Random House today, a much different business in a much different world.

When Random House went public a year after I arrived, its mood subtly changed. Bennett had always been a worrier. But now that Random House was listed, he would chew the corner of his white linen handkerchief in anguish whenever the stock fell. When the company had been his and Donald's, a slow season didn't matter. Next year or the year after would be better. Meanwhile the backlist kept the company afloat.

Eventually Random House stock, which had risen rapidly in the bull market for glamour issues, fell along with other publishing shares, and Bennett, who was now a national television celebrity, worried that his fans who had invested in the firm would think he didn't know his business. Like all celebrities, Bennett thrived on applause, which he imagined now depended upon rising quarterly profits, an impossible goal even for a firm as successful as Random House. A few fortuitous best-sellers distorted a year's profits so that the following year suffered by comparison. Publishers understood this pattern. Wall Street did not.

In his memoirs Bennett wrote that he and Donald had "deliberately passed up real wealth for the joy of doing what we wanted, and suddenly we were rich in spite of ourselves." But when they went public they no longer felt quite so free to do what they wanted. Bob Loomis, my friend and colleague of forty-two years, told me that Bennett used to come into his office to ask whether he was happy. I'm sure his interest in Bob's mood was genuine. But he was also, I suspect, asking for Bob's approval of his own performance as head of the firm. Now that we were his stockholders as well as his employees he had further reason to worry about our spirits. This was unnecessary. We never discussed the price of the stock, which Bennett and Donald had generously let us buy, in several cases with money borrowed from themselves, before it went public, and I doubt that any us worried about its ups and downs as Bennett did.

Bennett wrote in his memoirs that he and Donald went public in order to establish the firm's value for estate purposes, which was partly true. Another reason, apart from the money they stood to make, is that they were getting older and were thinking about who would succeed them. Knopf, Viking, Simon & Schuster, and the other so-called Jewish firms, were now mature businesses with substantial assets if the minimal and uncertain profits typical of the industry. By selling stock, Bennett and Donald had begun at long last to take their money out of the firm. They had also withdrawn in more subtle ways. Bennett was now famous, thanks to *What's My Line*, his weekly television show, and a highly paid lecturer. He spent weeks away from the office, defending his long absences on the road as good publicity for Random House and its authors. This was true. Much of the glamour that still attaches to Random House derives from Bennett's popularity. He was also a popular columnist and named his Mount Kisco weekend house The Columns in recognition of how he had paid for this expensive acreage, where at the pool uniformed maids and waiters in white coats served double-thick lamb chops and baked potatoes accompanied by little porcelain pots of ketchup. His joke books sold hundreds of thousands of copies. For the firm to survive, however, it needed a solid foundation, one that didn't depend on the fame, talent, and generosity of its aging founders.

This meant expansion, enough at any rate so that the founders could offer their eventual successors reasonable financial incentives. Expansion was unavoidable, but it diluted the intimacy and informality that had made my first years at Random House a delight. When Bennett and Donald ran the firm, our occasional staff meetings were chaotic. Donald would fuss with his pipe and stare otherwise motionless out the window onto Madison Avenue. Bennett, on the other hand, could not sit still. He told jokes, changed the subject, walked out, returned, told another joke, walked out again. But now our days were organized around meetings that Bennett and Donald didn't bother to attend. When RCA bought the firm, Bob Bernstein, Bennett's successor as president, did his best to sustain the old improvisational Random House style. He told bad jokes himself and insulated his colleagues from the five-year budgets and other corporate nonsense that the RCA engineers to whom Bob reported demanded. But by the mid-1970s, Random House had become a big business and felt like one. I preferred spending time at the Frick amid the Fragonards and Goyas or across town at the office of *The New York Review of Books,* whose battered furnishings and floors piled high with books were a relief from the increasingly formal atmosphere at the new Random House offices on Third Avenue.

A year after Random House went public, Donald and Bennett bought Knopf. Alfred was older than Donald and Bennett, and his son Pat had recently left the firm to start a business of his own. Alfred's wife, Blanche—his partner and most brilliant editor—was not well, and Alfred's decision to sell, which was shocking at the time, was in retrospect inevitable. When Blanche's condition worsened a few years later and she had only a day or so to live, she left a note for Alfred to read at Frank Campbell's on Madison Avenue, where a string quartet in black skirts and white blouses on a stage banked with camelias awaited her friends and family. She thanked everyone for taking the trouble to attend, apologized for disturbing them on a busy Monday morning, and hoped they would enjoy some music that she and Alfred liked. It was a fine publisher's characteristically stylish goodbye. So was Bennett's several years later when his friend Phyllis Newman sang show tunes at St. Paul's Chapel on the Columbia campus, where Bennett had been a friend and classmate of Richard Rodgers and Lorenz Hart and become addicted to the Broadway theater. Dozens of writers, publishers, and agents attended, and as we chatted afterward on that raw rain-swept morning in the shadow of Low Library I knew that we had said goodbye to more than a single great publisher and dear friend.

Chapter Four

Goodbye to All That

The talented young men and women who had started their firms in the 1920s and introduced the literature of modernism to American readers by risking their fortunes and their destiny on Faulkner and Joyce, Proust, Gide, Lawrence, Stein, Stevens, and Pound would soon be gone, and so would their highly personal, hand-crafted publishing styles. They were not, of course, the only distinguished publishers who flourished during the interwar years. There were also Harper and Scribner, whose list included Hemingway and Fitzgerald; Harcourt,

Brace, which published Eliot and several Bloomsbury writers; Macmillan and the Boston firms
Houghton Mifflin and Little, Brown; and W. W.
Norton with its translations of Freud and its fine
music list. But these long established firms would
also be caught up in the transformation already begun when I joined Random House in 1958. At first
the changes were imperceptible. Like my colleagues
I assumed that Random House in the early 1960s
was a fixed star within its universe. Only gradually
did I see that its universe was itself in flux.

From its origins nearly two centuries ago until
the 1960s, when the suburban migration and the
hegemony of the shopping mall radically altered the
retail market for books, the American publishing
industry had followed an historic pattern. Manuscripts were sent by publishers to a compositor to
be set in type—by hand until the invention in 1884
of linotype machines and three years later of
monotype, which melted lead, cast it as type, and
set copy mechanically. The type, fitted into a form,
was given to a printer and placed on a press, which
produced printed sheets that were then folded and
gathered into signatures, sewn together, and
bound: essentially the same procedure that had
prevailed since Gutenberg. The smell of ink and
hot metal that permeated the printing houses on

Varick Street where Random House printed some of its titles in the early 1960s would probably have been familiar to the Renaissance printers of Verona. By the early nineteenth century a few innovations had been introduced. Steam presses were invented in 1810 and in 1846 stereotype plates made it possible to produce longer runs at less cost per copy. Books were sent from the printer to the publisher's warehouse and from there shipped to retailers from whom the publisher's travelers had previously solicited orders. Some books—sets, for example, and expensive illustrated editions such as Audubon's *Birds of America*—were sold by subscription. But most books were sold in bookshops, which by the turn of the century were established in hundreds of cities and towns throughout the country.

A peculiarity of the trade has been the custom, established during the Depression of the 1930s, that unsold copies can be returned for full credit to the publishers. In effect, books are sold on consignment. Because it was usually impossible to know in advance whether a book would sell, booksellers could not afford to risk their precious capital on unknown authors without a publisher's indemnity. Rather than lose their customers to bankruptcy, publishers, following the practice introduced by Simon & Schuster, agreed to take unsold copies back for credit against future orders. "Gone today. Here tomorrow" was Alfred Knopf's comment on this grim condition of sale. Publishers have since learned to cover the cost of returns by inflating the retail price of books, so that book buyers pay not only for the copies they buy but a proportionate share of copies returned to publishers' warehouses to be destroyed and recycled. In the technological future, the problem of returns will be eliminated to the extent that books are printed on demand in response to customers' orders rather than printed in quantity and consigned to retail bookstores awaiting buyers who may or may not want them.

Harper Bros., one of the earliest American publishers, began as a New York printer in 1817. Soon the firm was competing with other New York printers to ship books, including pirated editions of British authors, via the Erie Canal to the hinterland, where local printers could not match New York prices. The canal gave the New York printers an advantage over their competitors in Boston and Philadelphia, which helps explain New York's pre-eminence as a book publishing center. There were, of course, other reasons. Boston was a Congregationalist theocracy with strong Puritan overtones, Philadelphia was a Quaker aristocracy. But New

York was polyglot, cosmopolitan, open to anyone with talent and ambition. John Jacob Astor, a fur trader, might have scraped by in Boston or Philadelphia. In New York he became, despite his lowly origins, his accent, and his foreign birth, the richest man in the United States and the founder of a dynasty. By the Civil War, New York's preeminence as a publishing center was well established.

The United States, with few writers of its own to protect and a printing industry to nurture, ignored international copyright throughout most of the nineteenth century. By 1853, Harper Bros., with a staff of five hundred, had become New York City's largest employer and the world's leading book publisher, having added Bibles and schoolbooks as well as books by American writers to its line of pirated works by Dickens, Thackeray, the Brontës, and others. According to Edwin G. Burrows and Mike Wallace in *Gotham*, their magisterial history of New York to 1898, surely the greatest and at nearly five pounds the most unwieldy history of a city ever written, Thomas Babbington Macaulay was the most successful of Harper's pirated authors. His *History of England from the Accession of James II* sold, according to Burrows and Wallace, an amazing 400,000 copies, a performance comparable to that of a major nonfiction best-seller today in a much larger America, to readers eager to outdo England's rise to world power.

By the 1840s the American market had become important enough for Charles Dickens to cross the Atlantic to protest the theft of his property. New York literary society held a ball in his honor for 2,500 guests at the Park Theatre, and Washington Irving was host at another dinner for a more select group at the City Hotel. But Dickens's plea for copyright protection was ignored, and by the time he left for Canada he had seen enough of the United States to be depressed by its rough edges. He recorded his disappointment in a short and uncharacteristically glum book—*American Notes*—which Harper immediately pirated and sold for 12½ cents a copy. *American Notes* is worth reading if only for its account of Dickens's journey by train from Washington to Philadelphia through what he thought was a storm of feathers but proved to be spit from the passengers in the forward coaches. American spitting offended Dickens. When he visited the Senate he complained that the senators spat so wide of the cuspidors that the carpets were like swamps. Soon after Dickens's unsuccessful appeal, American authors asked for protection for their own works in foreign editions, and by the end of the century Congress passed an International Copyright Act, to the benefit of publishers, who could now contract for exclusive rights to the works of British and other foreign writers and earn a normal profit from them.

By the mid-1850s, New York publishers were shipping millions of books to the hinterland. The most popular novel of the day, according to Burrows and Wallace, was *The Wide, Wide World,* written by an impoverished gentlewoman named Susan Warner. Harper rejected this "pious and sentimental" manuscript, calling it "fudge," but G. P. Putnam, alert to the genre then as now, picked it up and sold fourteen editions. In the decade before the Civil War there were 112 publishers in New York and others in Boston, Philadelphia, and other cities. New York had the advantage over these other cities, according to Burrows and Wallace, of a relatively carefree attitude toward "blood and thunder adventures, sado-masochistic romances laced with sex, horror and lurid accounts of patrician villainy and plebeian mischief," staples of the trade then as now. New York houses dominated the market for the genre until, in the 1870s, Anthony Comstock, a self-confessed former devotee of the solitary vice, convinced the city's leaders that for the sake of respectable appearances, a hypocritical electorate would not object to the suppression of its shameful fantasies. Major publishers thereafter catered to the genteel pretensions of readers who bowed to an idealized assumption of feminine modesty. It was not until the 1920s when publishers introduced the literature of modernism and its critique of all assumptions, that American publishing, to use Van Wyck Brooks's term, came of age along with the nation itself.

The 1920s were the golden age of American publishing, an age whose aura still glowed, if dimly, when I went to work for Doubleday. In 1950, the firms that were launched in the twenties were still small. When I joined Random House in 1958, its sales were just under $5 million, probably equal to Simon & Schuster's. Knopf and Viking were smaller. These houses were still run by their founders, and each had its own personality. From our perspective at Random House, Knopf and Viking had aged more than ourselves, while Simon & Schuster remained in a state of ageless adolescence. There were still thousands of privately owned bookshops in cities and towns everywhere. Most were barely as wide as a hallway, with such names as Smile-a-While and Book Nook and Bide-a-Wee, but many were dense with titles of all kinds, including regional and other special collections reflecting the interests of the owners. To linger in these shops for an hour or two was a bibliographic adventure amid the scent of bindings, where the accrued wisdom of the species was for sale, lined up on shelves alphabetically within the categories of thought. For the publishers and booksellers of the 1920s and after there were more than enough challenging new writers to make publishing a constant adventure. Irving, Cooper, and Twain had been celebrities in their day, but nothing like the writers who emerged in the interwar years and the postwar decades. When the proud publisher of *Forever Amber*, Kathleen Windsor's great best-seller of 1944, promoted her book with a glamorous portrait of its good-looking author, Bennett Cerf responded by taking an ad in the *Times* for Random House author Gertrude Stein, featuring a photograph of Miss Stein and Alice Toklas under the headline "We have glamour girls too."

When I entered the publishing business the postwar generation of promising American and European writers had begun to appear, and the retail marketplace of several thousand independent booksellers was well suited to the great variety of titles being published. I had no idea that this marketplace would soon crumble and collapse in a demographic shift whose premonitory rumblings could even then be heard if one's ears were better tuned than mine. In 1960 I edited for Random House *The Death and Life of Great American Cities,* Jane Jacobs's classic defense of urbanism against the powerful forces that threatened it, including the proponents of suburbia as a more wholesome environment than dense cities, but I failed to see the meaning of these forces for writers and publishers.

By the time I joined Random House the suburban migration was well advanced, but in New York readers could still buy current best-sellers and expensive sets at Macy's or at Scribner and Brentano's on Fifth Avenue, while in Greenwich Village and along upper Broadway near Columbia or on Fourth Avenue, as Park Avenue South was then called, booksellers stocked and readers from all over the city could choose from an infinite variety of more specialized titles, new and used. The pattern was the same in other cities. In New York and other cities many booksellers financed their slow-moving inventories by operating from premises they owned themselves, charging themselves no rent. Others set up shop in low-rent side streets and depended less on expensive, high-traffic locations than on customers who sought them out or who could be alerted by postal card or telephone to titles of interest. But as customers left for the suburbs, the owners abandoned these stores, at first by the score and then by the hundreds. Only a handful reopened in the suburbs, where the population was dispersed and shopping-mall rents were too high to sustain such eccentric, marginally profitable businesses with their large, often recondite backlist inventories and their perilously low rates of turnover. In bookselling as in any retail business, inventory and rent are a trade-off. The more you pay for one, the less you can spend on the other. Shopping-mall rents procluded the retail structure that had evolved hand in hand with the American publishing industry for nearly two centuries.

For publishers, the informal network of independent bookstores had been a sensitive gauge of an undulant and diverse literary marketplace, a primitive Internet that connected us intimately to the various communities of readers. This is not to say that publishers depended on the marketplace to shape their lists as film producers and politicians depend on focus groups and polls. But with the disappearance of the independent booksellers, publishers suffered a kind of sensory deprivation, a loss of contact with the external world. The result was a mild paranoia, a typical response to disorientation, as the retail marketplace, now concentrated in a new kind of bookstore adapted to the suburban malls, became mechanized and faceless, an undifferentiated force for which books were not precious or curious artifacts but stock-keeping units. By the 1970s my habitual daily calls to booksellers in various cities became less frequent and eventually came to an end.

Traditionally, department stores had subsidized their book departments as a convenience to attract customers. But when they moved to the malls, most department stores abandoned their unprofitable bookshops, counting on the mall itself to generate traffic. However, in 1969 two large Midwestern department store chains—Carter, Hawley, Hale and Dayton, Hudson—set their book departments up as freestanding chains, one called Waldenbooks and the other B. Dalton. These chains soon opened hundreds of uniform, centrally managed outlets, which greatly expanded, democratized, and soon dominated the market for books. But for this welcome expansion of the marketplace, publishers paid a high price. The mall stores radically altered the nature of publishing, for the iron rule by which inventory and rent are inverse reciprocals demanded high volume and high turnover. The mall bookstores were now paying the same rent as the shoe store next door and were bound by the same fiscal rules. They needed recognizable products that sold on impulse. This meant books by brand-name authors with their armies of loyal readers or by celebrities who pitched their books on the morning television shows and later on *Oprah*: royal princesses, health faddists, reformed mafiosi, discoverers of the twelve secrets of financial or romantic success, politicians, Eastern mystics, wrestlers, inspirational football coaches, body builders, diet doctors, gossips, evangelists, basketball stars, and so on. Meanwhile, publishers who for years had cultivated their backlists now found fewer accounts able to stock them.* The migration to the suburbs was splitting the industry into two quite different and incompatible businesses—a dominant one producing mass merchandise for the malls and another committed to the traditional search for backlist candidates.

---

* A change in the tax law affecting inventory valuation made it still more difficult for publishers to maintain extensive backlist inventories.

The model for mass-market publishing had been established in the 1930s and 1940s by the paperback houses—Pocket Books and its imitators—which distributed their titles monthly through magazine wholesalers primarily to newsstands and eventually to supermarkets and other mass outlets. Originally these wholesalers were national news distributors with branches in major cities. By the 1950s, independent distributors covering major suburban markets had replaced the city-based national wholesalers, and they too treated books as an adjunct to their magazine business. Since these paperbacks were usually cheap reprints of the previous year's best-sellers, the mass-market paperback publisher's editorial function was minimal, mainly a matter of selection and acquisition of published titles. Marketing was now the essential function and the editors at paperback houses were its servants, an inversion of the traditional relationship.

Since the supply of last year's best-sellers available for reprint was limited and increasingly expensive to acquire, the smaller mass-market houses solicited outside manuscripts directly from authors and marketed them as paperback originals in standard catagories—westerns, mysteries, romances, and so on. Some of these authors attracted their own loyal readers and were eventually sought out by hardcover houses. These writers, now marketed in hardcover editions, together with traditional hardcover brand-name writers, paid the rent for the mall stores and would eventually do the same for the so-called superstores that succeeded them. Inevitably the more commercially oriented hardcover houses assumed the characteristics of paperback mass marketers. While their editors remained generally loyal to their traditional function, marketing considerations now dominated the publishing operations at these firms, to the disadvantage of the wide range of titles too specialized or speculative to be promoted and sold to the chains. These titles were—and are—often left to fend for themselves.

Many find their way nevertheless, especially those that can be assigned in university courses or that attract their own groups of specialized readers. The dominance within today's publishing houses of marketing specialists and the chains they cater to is not absolute. Some so-called midlist books become great best-sellers in mysterious ways without the support of the chains in the first instance, for example, John Berendt's *Midnight in the Garden of Good and Evil*, whose perceptive editor published it with flair, and its sales expanded outward from the independent stores as if by nuclear fission as readers recommended it to their friends. Eventually the chains stocked it and it became a historic best-seller. *Midnight* sold more than two million copies, while many other midlist books sell in the hundreds of thousands despite the limitations of the overconcentrated retail marketplace. In the technological future, readership of such books will expand as authors, with the help of editors and publicists, and no longer constrained by the turnover requirements of a physical marketplace, present their work directly to readers over the World Wide Web, where word of mouth is instantaneous, credible, and widespread. Publishers had welcomed television as a powerful tool to promote their titles to the mass market created by the malls. But television is a one-way medium addressed to an undifferentiated audience to which access is at the discretion of the broadcaster. The Internet, by connecting readers and writers one on one, offers the possibility of almost limitless choice and foreshadows a literary culture thrilling if also alarming in its potential diversity.

Storytelling—transmitting the wisdom and history of the tribe through word, gesture, and song—is an innate human function that flourished long before the modern publishing industry existed and will flourish long after it is gone. The publishing industry, constrained by obsolete technologies and a constricted marketplace, now implements the transmission from writer to reader poorly. But prospective new technologies foreshadow the possibility of a reconstructed industry, one that will, I believe, perform its historic task with unprecedented scope and unimaginable consequences. Given the mottled history of our species, one should not assume a future of unmixed joy, but there are grounds for optimism nonetheless.

CHAPTER FIVE

Culture Wars

Partly through my friends from Columbia and Barbara's from Harvard and because of my search for titles to add to the Anchor series, Barbara and I found ourselves by the end of the 1950s in the midst of what would eventually be known as the New York intellectual community and a comparable group that came to be called the New York school of poets and artists. Enough has been written about this lower Manhattan Bloomsbury that I hesitate to add more. To Barbara and me at the time, its members were simply the gifted and argumentative writers and editors associated with *Partisan Review:* Robert Lowell and his wife, Elizabeth Hardwick; Will Barrett, whose useful introduction to existentialism, *Irrational Man,* I published; Dwight Macdonald and Fred Dupee, whom I also published; Hannah Arendt, the Trillings, Clement Greenberg, Mary McCarthy, and so on.

Partisan Review, where Barbara had worked for a while, had performed two indispensable services since its founding in the 1930s as an organ of the John Reed Clubs, a component of the Young Communist League. A year later it broke with communism and commenced its critique of Stalinism, a courageous heresy at the time. *Partisan's* circulation was negligible but its influence was enormous. For the next two decades it shaped the critique in the United States of Soviet communism while it also introduced the writers and issues associated with modernism in literature and art to American readers. *Partisan* led if it did not actually create America's intellectual discourse during the war years and after, until it lost its bearings in the moral and intellectual chaos of the Vietnam War and the cultural upheavals of the 1960s.

This intellectual world, which had once been united in its criticism of Stalinism and its defense of modernism—the issues are, of course, related: the victory of Stalinism would mean the end of art and literature—now broke into polemical factions over various Cold War issues. Should criticism of American culture be muted, lest it help the Soviet Union and its propagandists, or is such criticism an essential function within a democracy? Could Senator McCarthy be defended, despite his Red-baiting, for having alerted Americans to the threat of domestic communism? How serious was this threat? And what should be done about the Soviet cultural offensive? Should intellectuals respond by accepting covert funding from the CIA to support publications that promoted our positions? Was it right for those in the know to deceive their fellow writers about these connections? Was the Vietnam War a defense of American interests or a trap from which politicians, afraid of attacks from the right, lacked the courage to extricate us?

These were legitimate and even urgent questions, but the debate became parochial and personal. Dr. Johnson said somewhere that literary criticism should not partake of "impertinent autobiography." What a critic likes or dislikes is an irrelevant personal confession, like preferring the color green to blue or Stilton to cheddar. The relevant question is how the cheese was made, whether it is sharp or mild, edible or toxic. But important questions were now framed as *ad hominem* attacks and justified metaphysically as the defense of "Western Culture," as if contrary opinions were not simply other points of view but insults to the civilization we all shared. The intellectual community whose critique of Stalinism and defense of modernism had been heroic was now disintegrating in the face of issues beyond its moral and intellectual grasp. Its more sophisticated members drifted away, while those who remained clung to various orthodoxies with passionate, often infantile, intensity.

In December 1962, workers at *The New York Times* went on strike. By now Barbara and I were living on West 67th Street in one of those romantic apartments built for artists at the turn of the century, with two-story living rooms and north-facing windows from chair rail to ceiling: an adult version of my bohemian attic on Tenth Street. A balcony hung over the living room, the fireplace mantels were intricately molded, and the walls were paneled in wood. In 1913 the Armory Show of avant-garde art, which featured Marcel Duchamp's *Nude Descending a Staircase,* included works from the Arensberg collection that had been assembled in this building in

1907. Our friends the Lowells lived in a similar apartment on the same block. At first we lived there without furniture, but by now we had enough chairs to invite friends for a meal. One evening during the second week of the strike the Lowells and we were finishing our coffee when I asked whether they agreed that the world seemed to have become much smaller without the *Times*. Sixty-seventh Street had become a village, remote from the outside world. I added that the absence of the *Times Book Review* was a further blessing.

To put the problem of the *Times Book Review* at that time most charitably, its editors had not adjusted to the sophisticated generation of postwar, college-educated readers. Its reviews were ill-informed, bland, occasionally spiteful, usually slapdash. Authors lived in terror that their books would be assigned to a reviewer who had no idea what they were saying. In an article Elizabeth Hardwick had just written for our friend Bob Silvers, who was then an editor at *Harper's Magazine,* she put the case powerfully: "The flat praise and the faint dissension," she wrote, "the minimal style and the light little article, the absence of involvement, passion, character, eccentricity—the lack of the literary tone itself—have made *The New York Times Book Review* a provincial journal."

The strike offered a chance—indeed, it imposed the obligation, given our complaints—to publish a review that represented those qualities that Lizzie found lacking in the *Times*. No one said as much that evening, but perhaps we were also thinking of an alternative to *Partisan Review*, which in its middle age had also become provincial. The strike left us no choice. Either we seize the opportunity or stop complaining.

The next morning Lowell borrowed $4,000 from his trust fund. The idea was to publish a single issue during the strike and decide later whether to continue. My own position was complicated. Though Bennett and Donald had agreed that I could start businesses of my own, I could hardly become involved editorially in a paper that would review Random House and Knopf books and those of their competitors, nor could I expect Bennett and Donald to become involved financially should we decide upon regular publication. While Lowell was negotiating his loan, I told Bennett and Donald what we had in mind. "Keep your distance editorially," Donald said, "and everything should be fine." Bennett told a joke about some people in Beverly Hills and that ended the discussion.

That afternoon we called our brilliant friend

Bob Silvers, who agreed to take a leave from *Harper's*, whose editor told him that the world didn't need another literary magazine and that he'd soon be back at his job. With Elizabeth Hardwick's help, Bob and Barbara would edit the special issue and sell ads to publishers, who, because of the strike, had no other place to advertise their new titles. By the end of the week, Barbara and Bob had sold $10,000 worth of ads, and these commitments guaranteed the printer's fee. Meanwhile the distributor who sold Anchor Books to campus bookstores and newsstands agreed to take 100,000 copies. Bob and Barbara set up their editorial office at Bob's desk at *Harper's* and I stayed away.

However, in setting up the business I made two important suggestions: first, that if we decided upon regular publication, the founders—Bob, Barbara, the Lowells, and I—would own all the voting shares (eventually we offered shares to Whitney Ellsworth, who became our publisher), and second, that the review would pay its own way. *Partisan, The New Republic, The Nation,* and similar magazines depended upon rich patrons whose prejudices had to be taken into account by the editors. We would preserve our independence by being profitable. I calculated that by keeping our costs down and operating in a business-like way, we could do so.

The Lowells, Bob, Barbara, and I shared certain values but had no ideological position or political program.* We valued literature, the other arts, and science as the greatest human achievements. We believed that good writers could make almost any subject interesting and intelligible and bore the obligation to do so within their powers; that official points of view and government activities should be viewed skeptically; and that human rights abuses whether inflicted by Communists, fascists, religious fanatics, or ourselves should be exposed. We opposed the Soviet Union as well as the war in Vietnam. We also opposed capital punishment as an act of vengeance, unworthy of a great country and an insult to the sanctity of life. But these preferences were the implicit basis of our friendship and not elements of a political or ideological program.

In Bob's office, surrounded by piles of books submitted for review, Lizzie, Barbara, and Bob

---

* Some readers have discerned an implicit ideological bias on the part of *The New York Review,* but this may be a reflection of their own intellectual commitments. The *Review* has always been skeptical of doctrine except as noted below.

drew up a list of writers who might wish to write for the paper we had in mind. These writers represented the level of discourse that the *Review* aimed for and has attempted to maintain ever since. They included Edmund Wilson, Richard Wilbur, Roger Shattuck, Alfred Kazin, V. S. Pritchett, Fred Dupee, W. H. Auden, Dwight Macdonald, and fifty or sixty others on whom the editors would depend if the reception of the special issue encouraged them to proceed. What these writers had in common was their eclectic curiosity and their ability to make difficult subjects intelligible to general readers. Whatever their special interests might be, they were, for the purposes of *The New York Review of Books,* as we decided to call our paper, journalists: skeptical, open-minded, objective.

As the strike continued, the first edition of *The New York Review* was printed and shipped. The leading article was an appreciative review by Fred Dupee of James Baldwin's *The Fire Next Time.* Dupee admired Baldwin's prose and respected his passion but disliked his threatened apocalypse, a judgment that has held up over time. The first issue also included an unfriendly review of *The Centaur,* a novel by John Updike, an important Knopf author. Knopf's publicity director at the time considered this treason on my part and recommended to Alfred that I be fired. The publicity director subsequently chose another career and Updike eventually became an important contributor to *The New York Review*. A week after the special issue was shipped we received the first of two thousand letters urging that we continue. Since we printed only 100,000 copies, not all of which could have been distributed, this was a phenomenal response that would have stunned the direct marketers at Doubleday. We decided to do a second experimental issue in the fall. If that went well, without benefit of the strike, we would raise the capital to proceed biweekly. In all we raised $145,000, all of it in exchange for nonvoting shares.

Salaries were minimal, the newsprint was cheap, the offices at 57th and Broadway were cramped and the furniture secondhand. Bob and Barbara worked together into the night and on weekends, and by the third year *The New York Review* became profitable, and has remained so, the only publication of its kind, I believe, ever to operate in the black year after year. Eventually we started a book club for gardeners and bought another club addressed to serious readers as insurance should *The New York Review* run short of cash. But this never happened.

Today, some thirty-seven years later, Bob and Barbara still work into the night and on weekends and the few original contributors who survive continue to write for it, while those who are gone have been replaced by such younger writers as Ian Buruma, Luke Menand, Pankaj Mishra, Geoffrey O'Brien, and Timothy Garton Ash, among many others. The *Review* made many friends and many enemies. Philip Rahv, the famously gruff and brilliant coeditor of *Partisan Review,* became an important friend of *The New York Review.* His partner, a sweet-tempered man named William Phillips, nevertheless fired me from *Partisan's* advisory board, a meaningless snub since the board's only function was to raise money for the chronically impoverished magazine.

It had not occurred to me that Random House and Knopf authors would not always welcome what was written about their books in *The New York Review* until some of my own authors were criticized. Even now, years later, I feel the pain inflicted by these reviews. James Thurber in *The New Yorker* once compared the dismay on a man's face to that of Albert Payson Terhune, the author of *Lassie,* and other sheepdog classics, upon being bitten by a collie. This is how I felt, but I said nothing, nor did the aggrieved writers. Nonetheless, *The New York Review's* right-wing opponents, especially during the Vietnam War, accused the *Review's* writers of favoring one another's books, but these comments were tendentious and easily ignored, as were the more sinister comments during the war that the *Review* was leftist, un-American, culturally subversive, and so on.

In the same year that I joined Random House I became involved briefly and peripherally with the CIA. A friend who worked for the agency invited me to accompany him as a consultant to West Africa, where the CIA was considering whether to fund an American-oriented elementary school textbook program for Nigerian and Ghanaian children. At the time the Soviets were active in Ghana, and the agency seemed to fear that the schools in the region would be flooded with anti-American propaganda. The fear was groundless. The British controlled the market for West African schoolbooks, and their product was far better than anything we or the Russians could supply. Our trip was enjoyable but a waste of time. We drank palm wine and ate groundnut stew. We spent afternoons on the beach. We drove into the interior. I taught the bartender at the Federal

Palace Hotel in Lagos to make dry martinis. But the British were in command of the elementary schools and neither we nor the Russians were going to supplant them.

My friend, however, had larger plans for Africa. He was determined that African youth not succumb to Stalinism and had previously arranged with the government of South Africa to allow young African intellectuals to accept fellowships, sponsored by the Agency, to attend British and American universities. The condition was that they not return to South Africa when their fellowships expired. My friend truly believed that he was offering these young intellectuals a chance at a better life. In fact he was conspiring with the South African regime to exile its potential opponents permanently. On a wintry Thanksgiving morning our friend invited Barbara and me to his apartment on the edge of Harlem for a drink. When we arrived his place was in chaos, the windows open, the floor a mess. We stood in the doorway without removing our coats. Our friend was in worse condition than his apartment. He had been drinking but managed to tell us that during the night one of his young South Africans who had come down from Harvard to stay with him for the weekend had thrown himself from a window onto the icy pavement and was dead.

How, I wondered, did this poor exile's death advance the cause that my friend thought he was defending? How, on a greater scale, did our blundering in Vietnam advance the American cause there?

CHAPTER SIX

Groves of Academe

The great expansion of college enrollments that followed World War Two produced a classless generation of serious readers to whom both Anchor Books and *The New York Review of Books* were addressed. This generation marked a real split with the past. The GI Bill had democratized higher education and liberated it from its aristocratic tradition. One consequence of this new intellectual diversity was the discovery that American writers of the nineteenth century were not provincial relics of a genteel past but bold critics, in many cases, of a past that had itself been anything but quaint. When I attended Columbia College in the 1940s, American literature was taught only in a single course by Quentin Anderson. But under the influence of D. H. Lawrence, Perry Miller, Van Wyck Brooks, F. O. Mathiessen, Newton Arvin, Edmund Wilson, Alfred Kazin, F. W. Dupee, Lionel Trilling, and other writers, American literature would soon become an academic industry, and decent editions of long-neglected American writers would be needed.

One mild autumn afternoon when Random House was still in the Villard mansion, I walked ten blocks south to meet Edmund Wilson for drinks at the old Princeton Club on Park Avenue just south of Grand Central Terminal. I was early, as usual, and took a seat at the bar. When Wilson arrived, wearing his crushed fedora and what his friend Scott Fitzgerald called his habitual tan raincoat, he ordered a half-dozen martinis. Thinking one or two of these might be intended for me, I ordered nothing. When the drinks arrived, arranged by the bartender, obviously familiar with Wilson's preference, in a kind of phalanx, Wilson turned to me and asked whether I would like a half-dozen too. I said no, and then, having disposed of the amenities, he announced in

his abrupt way that Americans ought to have editions
of their writers comparable to those published by
the Pléiade, the French series of compact, uniform
editions of the major and in many cases the complete works of important French writers.

Wilson did not have to tell me that American
writers were barely in print: paperback editions
intended for classrooms of *Moby-Dick, The Scarlet
Letter,* and *Huckleberry Finn* could be found, but
American readers had nothing comparable to the
compact French editions or the editions of standard British authors published by Oxford and
Cambridge. Even the Russians had done better by
their native literature, insofar as the censors permitted, than we had done. What Wilson envi-
sioned was a series of plump volumes of modest
height—like himself, he said—printed on thin,
acid-free paper and flexibly bound, a series that
would eventually comprise all of American literature worth having. He hoped the volumes could
be made to fit into the pocket of a raincoat like
the one he was wearing, from which he withdrew a
volume of the Pléiade Flaubert, laying it on the
bar beside the one remaining martini.

This seemed to me a splendid and urgent idea,

but I did not feel that such a project could be financed commercially. In the early 1960s it was still possible to assume that the more popular authors might be stocked by a thousand or more retailers and pay their way, but the object of the series was to be inclusive. This meant that over time, substantial, slow-moving inventories would accumulate and have to be supported on a nonprofit basis. The entire series could probably not be stocked in more than a few hundred bookstores—a vast overestimate, as I would eventually learn. By the time the Library of America finally appeared in the mid-1980s there probably weren't twenty retailers, if that many, likely to display every volume.

In the following weeks, Wilson and I drew up lists of authors to be included, roughed out a format based on the Pléiade but with cloth, not leather, bindings, and created a fund-raising prospectus to be submitted to foundations. The prospectus was endorsed by a committee of sponsors that included many of the important American critics and writers of the day as well as by President Kennedy, in words composed for the President, I suspect, by our friend Arthur Schlesinger, Jr., who served in Kennedy's White House. What we omitted from our list of sponsors, not on principle but because we did not know of their existence, were representatives of an obscure group of university professors who had made a specialty of establishing accurate texts of the work of American and British writers. This omission, of no consequence in itself, was a political error which would delay the project for a quarter century. Oblivious to our error, I approached people at the major foundations, none of whom were interested in what Wilson and I had in mind. Our problem, I soon discovered, was that few of our illustrious sponsors had the correct academic credentials and none represented an established academic organization. Our amateur status had frightened the foundations, and their response was to pretend that our project, which would eventually become the Library of America, made no sense or didn't fit their agendas. It was after several such rejections that I became aware that a subgroup of textual scholars with a publishing plan of their own and the support of the Modern Language Association was the source of our problem.

When the textual scholars heard of Wilson's plan, they warned the National Endowment for the Humanities, then in its bureaucratic infancy, that only their special techniques and complicated collating machines could solve the innumerable textual problems that afflicted American literature, and that Wilson and I, who lacked their arcane knowledge, would only make matters worse if we went forward on our own. In fact, the editorial task was not a matter of archaeological recovery as it was for the Anchor Bible. Competent editors capable of analyzing variant readings could solve all but the most baffling textual problems, and these could probably not be solved by anyone. Wilson, who was adept at this kind of work in connection with his critical writing, had anticipated the textual situation and knew several competent textual editors in New York, not affiliated with the academic group, who could be depended upon to sort out variant readings. Had the professors been interested in the propagation of accurate texts, they might have offered to cooperate with, rather than oppose, Wilson and me. Had they done so, the Library of America could have been published in the mid-sixties, rather than a quarter century later. Instead the professors persuaded the National Endowment for the Humanities to finance their own editions, produced at great expense and consisting of page after page of variant readings, many of them trivial, some of them mystifying, others helpful, that obscured the texts themselves so that it was occasionally difficult to tell what the authors had actually written.

In 1968, Wilson wrote *The Fruits of the MLA*, an angry pamphlet, published by *The New York Review of Books*, that was severely critical of the academic scholars who, he felt, had hijacked the funding for his project. While acknowledging that textual problems existed, Wilson demolished their version of the severity of these problems and their claim that only they with their special machinery and techniques could supply the correct readings. As an example of their work, Wilson mentioned the eighteen scholars who were assigned to read *Tom Sawyer* aloud backward so as not to be diverted by the story or Twain's style as they looked for misprints. The professor who told Wilson about this absurd behavior was himself on the payroll of the Twain project and cheerfully admitted that it was a "boondoggle," thinking that Wilson was sufficiently *au courant* with academic practice to appreciate this ingenious scheme to extract funds from foundations. But Wilson did not sympathize with this aspect of academic life and was not amused.

Undaunted, in fact exhilarated, by our setback and convinced, naively, that the absurdity of the heavily annotated editions would soon become apparent to the NEH (we were, of course, mistaken), Wilson and I renewed our campaign. When Wilson died in 1972, I carried on alone. Meanwhile, a new complication had arisen. Wilson's angry pamphlet not only had publicized his conflict with the textual scholars but had questioned the wisdom of the Modern Language Association. Foundation executives were now less inclined than ever to take Wilson's side against this powerful bureaucracy.

In the years after Wilson's death I came to know an official at the Ford Foundation named Roger Kennedy, an unusual member of his trade who later became a distinguished American historian. He was intrigued by Wilson's plan and described it to McGeorge Bundy, who was then about to retire as president of the Ford Foundation. As a parting favor to Bundy, Ford's trustees agreed to contribute $500,000 toward Wilson's project provided the NEH matched this sum. Bundy, with whom I sharply disagreed over Vietnam, was nonetheless a highly intelligent man with a powerful sense of duty and remarkable political skills. I admired him despite our differences, and we became good friends.

He agreed to negotiate with the NEH and assigned me the task of adding what he called "plenty of academic window dressing" to our application for funds.

Since I was a commercial publisher, and still worse, Wilson's representative on earth, Bundy recommended that I remain out of sight as much as possible. My presence, he warned me, would give the professors an excuse to "dive-bomb" the staff at the NEH as they had done in Wilson's day. I agreed with Bundy and felt that because of Wilson's pamphlet the NEH staff would be more wary of our project than ever. I regretted that Ford had put us in the hands of the NEH but knew that it had done so to legitimize its own commitment to what must have seemed, even then, a daring project.

I followed Bundy's advice and arranged the window dressing, which included a former high official of the Modern Language Association, so that I was barely visible amid the half-dozen or so academic politicians who had joined our team. We included among our camouflage a textual scholar who, now that he was on our side, agreed that the project's editors could safely rely upon the best texts available during the authors' lifetime and refer any further problems to an appropriate scholar. This sensible approach had been Wilson's original plan.*

Several meetings ensued between Bundy, a sampling of our professors, and me on one side and on the other Joe Duffy, the chairman of the National Endowment for the Humanities, and his staff. At the final and decisive meeting the staff were impossible to read. At previous meetings they had been affable, though we knew that their affability was disingenuous. If the NEH matched Ford, their budgets would be reduced accordingly. As Mac and I entered Chairman Duffy's office, his program officers were standing so close together that they might have been holding hands. They grinned, looked at the ceiling or the floor, coughed, exchanged among themselves inscrutable facial signals, offered to fetch coffee or take our coats, uttered other pleasantries, but the fox had finally got into their coop and their affability on this day barely hid their panic. Their chairman moved back and forth between them and us, whispering to one

---

* The Library of America editions also benefited from the textual work of the scholars who had originally opposed Wilson's project.

staff member, patting another on the back, while keeping his eye on Bundy, who stood with arms crossed, beaming with anticipation, awaiting the decision. It was obvious that the chairman hoped to avoid a confrontation with an opponent whose legendary bureaucratic power arose from years of enthusiasm for the task, and from his links to both political parties as well as to Ford and other powerful foundations. It was also obvious that Duffy's staff strongly opposed our application.

It had been snowing heavily all day. The airports were closed. Bundy and I had less than an hour to get to Union Station and catch a Metroliner so that we could be in New York in time for our dinner appointments. Suddenly the scene in the chairman's office seemed to unfold all at once, as in a dream or a car crash. As the chairman continued to stride from one end to the other of his row of underlings, Bundy thrust out his hand, reminding Duffy of the snow, the lateness of the hour, the withdrawal of Ford's grant unless the NEH matched it, the fact that there would be no second chances. "Let's settle this now," Bundy said with the same bright smile that he had maintained throughout the meeting.

The chairman, returning his smile, backed away

from Bundy's outstretched arm into the row of NEH officers behind him. Trapped physically as well as bureaucratically between Bundy and his own staff, Duffy halted. He opened his mouth but made no sound. It didn't matter. Bundy lunged forward, took Duffy's hand in both of his, pumped it once, and said, "Good. We have a deal."

Duffy smiled, but whether in agony or relief was unclear. Mac was already in his overcoat as he shook the hand of each offical in turn, congratulating them all on their decision. They too smiled, and so the deal was struck. I found my coat, and together we rode down the elevator, saying nothing. Mac's complexion was ruddy, as usual, and his eyes twinkled behind his glasses. It was impossible in the elevator to know whether he was pleased with his victory or simply beaming in anticipation of our next challenge: the race to the train through a blizzard that had halted every car on Connecticut Avenue.

Thanks to Mac Bundy, the Library of America now exists exactly as Wilson had conceived it twenty-five years previously in the Princeton Club bar. The irreproachable texts are complete and appear without footnotes or introductions, as he intended. The volumes are short, plump, and well made, like him, and fit neatly into a raincoat pocket. The series is a permanent monument to his vision and persistence, though he is nowhere acknowledged as its progenitor.

In keeping with Bundy's advice, I remained a somewhat ghostly presence at the Library of America while I arranged the details of design, format, production, and distribution as well as the financial structure. Editorial selection and style would follow Wilson's original plan precisely. The professors and the manager we had hired knew nothing about publishing and refrained from interfering while I set the project up. The Library of America was well received, and with luck it appeared that our original grant would last until the series could safely be turned over to a university press with a sufficient endowment to keep the series in print and support a small editorial staff to produce four new volumes a year until the Library had accomplished the goal Wilson had set. This would be a better and far less expensive way to guarantee long-term stability, I felt, than to maintain a separate organization with its own offices, salaries, stipends, and so on. The model I had in mind was the Loeb Classical Library, successfully managed for years by the Harvard University Press. The professors and staff strongly opposed this idea.

At the Princeton Club, Wilson and I had discussed the possibility of eventually adding to the series volumes on American art and architecture and even industrial design. I pursued this notion for several months, but concluded that our staff was not capable of handling such an ambitious scheme.

Within three years the Library of America had become a respected institution. By this time the academic group that I had assembled at Bundy's suggestion had overcome its initial reticence and had begun soliciting funds for projects that didn't meet the high editorial standard of the Library of America. Though I had only a single vote on the board I strongly objected to this activity. Harsh words were exchanged, and I left the board without regrets.

The editorial selection has followed Wilson's original prospectus but with troubling deviations. These include a volume of sermons *most of which are without* literary value or historical interest in themselves; collections of first-hand descriptions by journalists of American battles, interesting in themselves but of little interest as literature; the novels in translation of Vladimir Nabokov who is no more an American writer than Joseph Brodsky is an American poet; and a four-volume anthology of American poetry, separately financed by the National Endowment for the Humanities, which includes, inexplicably, much that is second rate or worse. A single volume devoted to the important poetry of the nineteenth century and a more substantial volume of twentieth-century American poetry would have been preferable, though perhaps insufficiently grandiose to justify a grant from the Endowment. A hint of similar trouble ahead is the announcement of a forthcoming anthology of writing by Americans about *oceans*, separately financed by a generous donor. Since the aim of the Library of America is to make permanently available the complete or substantially complete works of important American writers, this topical anthology represents not only a dilution of purpose but a waste of scarce resources, and it may foreshadow a future fund-raising effort in which other well-meaning, if naive, millionaires are approached to sponsor anthologies, bearing their names, dealing with such other aspects of nature as mountains, rivers, lakes, and more. Hospitals and libraries raise funds by appealing in a similar way to the vanity of donors. But topical anthologies, unlike hospital wards and reading rooms, are of little value in themselves. They serve no literary pupose, usually find few readers and quickly go out of print. Moreover, readers who *may* want to know what writers have said about oceans and other natural systems are ill served by an anthology whose principle of selection is constrained by the national identity of its contributors. The Libary of America has now published substantially all the work for which it was created and for which rights are available. Its obligation hereafter is to husband its resources so that this work remains in print and accessible to readers, and to ensure that funds are on hand for the publication of twentienth-century writers as rights permit.

As of June 30, 1999, the Library of America had assets of $8,500,000 of which $4,500,000 were in cash and investments. Its gross margin for that fiscal year from sales of $6,600,000, after deducting manufacturing and royalty expenses, was $4,300,000. Of this sum, some $2,300,000 was spent on sales and promotion, leaving $2,000,000 to cover fixed costs which in normal circumstances would provide a substantial surplus. Of these fixed costs, however, the largest item was $1,750,000 for salaries and rent on two floors in midtown Manhat-

tan, or more than $400,000 for each of the four
titles, consisting of reprinted material by established writers, published by the Library of America
annually. Of this remarkable sum, five of the twelve
directors received $600,000 exclusive of benefits.
Nearly half of this amount went to the Chairman of
the Board and the President. These and related
overhead items absorbed the entire $2,000,000.
However, grants and gifts of $770,000 provided a
surplus for the year of $780,000. By contracting
with a university press for basic housekeeping services, the Library of America could elminate many
of these overhead items and assure itself a long and
serene life under a small editorial staff and an un-
paid board. Without additional fund raising, the
Library of America would then contribute a posi-
tive cash flow of about $1,000,000 annually to its
already substantial assets.

Twenty-five years after Wilson first proposed
what would become the Library of America, there
was little room in the shopping-mall chains for
these tidy volumes of Emerson, James, Melville,
and eventually nearly sixty other American writers.
The thousand or so bookstores that I had hoped
would stock the more popular titles had all but disappeared. Therefore I arranged with a direct-

marketing friend from Doubleday who was now in charge of Time-Life Books to sell the series by subscription. The success of this direct-mail campaign and strong sales through *The New York Review*'s book club revealed a substantial market for these books, but one that could no longer be reached through retail booksellers. The Internet existed, but its commercial possibilities were as yet invisible. Had the Library of America been launched ten years later I would probably have promoted and sold it on the World Wide Web, its natural venue.

CHAPTER SEVEN

Modern Times

My first hint of what would eventually become the Internet occurred in the late 1950s, when I still worked at Doubleday and published an Anchor edition of a book called *The Human Use of Human Beings* by Norbert Wiener, a professor of electrical engineering at MIT. Wiener had been a child prodigy who entered Tufts College at the age of eleven and received his Ph.D. in mathematics from Harvard at eighteen. For forty years he taught at MIT, where he acquired a reputation for eccentricity. But this reputation misrepresented the range and quality of his mind, which had a strong poetic component. In the 1950s, Wiener became suddenly famous as the author of an unlikely best-seller—a book called *Cybernetics*. This was a fairly technical discussion of so-called feedback mechanisms as they function in computers and in the human brain. He did not believe that the two phenomena were literally analogous but that they exemplified in different ways self-correcting feedback systems of which the environment as a whole was yet another example. In this prophetic book Wiener explained how the electronic on-off switches in computers swiftly calculate complex variables and how something similar happens in the brain when we reach, for example, for a moving object, say a tennis ball. We do not grasp the ball directly but increasingly (and in split seconds) narrow the error of our reach in response to digital signals from the synapses of the brain. The analogy Wiener used in his conversations with me was that of an artillery-man bracketing his target in response to yes/no signals from his spotter.

Wiener knew something about artillery. In the interwar years he had offered to build for the army an antiaircraft gun—pointing mechanism based on an experimental computer design that he was developing. Wiener was a pacifist, but he felt that the many variables involved in aiming the gun—the speed and evasive maneuvers of the enemy plane, the direction and velocity of the wind, the design of the aiming mechanism, imperfections in the gears, and so on—provided an opportunity to test the high-speed electronic switches he had designed to replace the mechanical systems used in the primitive computing devices of that period. Later, when the army decided to adopt his gun-pointing device, Wiener complained that he had been misled. He did not want his work to be used to kill people. He complained to the army but was ignored. It was from such episodes that Wiener's reputation for eccentricity grew.

Wiener coined the title of his best-seller, whose first two syllables have since become ubiquitous and lost their meaning, from the Greek word for steersman. His idea was that self-regulating feedback mechanisms in search of equilibrium are analogous to the steersman adjusting his tiller in response to the flow of air and water, the weight and balance of the boat, and other unpredictable variables. The implicit moral lesson for the environment is that inappropriate actions will stimulate unwanted responses: a helmsman who oversteers will swamp the boat; a city that poisons its air will sicken and die; a rigid society or individual unable to process new information will fail. Wiener was an early environmentalist who warned that nature could be pushed only so far before it pushed back. His warning about rigid systems unable to process new information would become for me a metaphor for the overconcentrated retail book market and the implicit censorship such a market imposed upon the self-correcting process of unmediated discussion.

I looked forward to my visits with Wiener in Cambridge and his speculation about what these new electronic feedback mechanisms, whose circuitry he helped develop, might lead to. Wiener was a smiling man, plump as a medicine ball with arms and legs too short for this body. He wore a three-piece suit woven of something like iron, a specialty of Boston tailors in those days. Because Wiener suffered from very poor eyesight he could see where he was going only by tilting his head up to peer over the tops of the thick, black frames of his glasses. As a result he seemed to be gazing at distant planets as we walked across the MIT campus toward the luncheonette where he ordered his habitual midday meal, a carton of milk and a bag of potato chips. He was notoriously absentminded. He is said to have flustered his colleagues by wandering into their classrooms to scribble on their blackboards while they were lecturing. But his eccentricities were superficial. Powerful metaphors linking his theoretical work to the visible world flowed easily from his mind. Unlike many scientists who imagine the world in the language of mathematics, Weiner was able to convey his ideas in ordinary language with unusual clarity.

It was from Wiener in the 1950s that I first heard of the second law of thermodynamics, which posits the inexorable deterioration of closed systems in nature as their temperatures become increasingly uniform with that of their surroundings over time. There is nothing arcane about this law: an unstoked fire will burn itself out, and when it does, the temperature of its ashes will soon be indistinguishable from that of the surrounding atmosphere. The same is true of myself when I too can no longer assimilate energy and become dust. According to the law, both dust and atmosphere will eventually devolve into random molecules, which will deteriorate in turn until all energy has flowed from the system and all temperature is uniform. The measure of this deterioration is called entropy. Because the second law foretells the hypothetical end of everything, including the presumably finite universe and all its innumerable suns, entropy soon took on a life of its own in the minds of postwar Hamlets. Entropy stood for the self-proclaimed impoverishment of their own isolated lives in suburban America, cut off from external sources of vitality. In cosmological terms, this terminal uniformity of temperature as the universe expends its irreplaceable energy is known as "the heat death," and this term too became a metaphor for life in the 1950s.

In the electromagnetic terms that interested Wiener, entropy also measures the loss of information transmitted over a wire or through the atmosphere as signals weaken and disintegrate over time into noise and eventually silence, unless new energy is fed into the system. But Wiener was an optimist. In the hypothetical very long run, the universe will die as all temperatures are extinguished in the undifferentiated heat death. In the meantime, however, there is life, which creates order and meaning. The metaphor that Wiener used to illustrate the second law was a salmon swimming upriver to spawn new life. As the river flows into the sea and loses its identify along with its distinctive temperature, the salmon fights its way upstream, temporarily creating new meaning, new order, new life. Though the salmon will eventually return to the sea and die, its struggle stands for the temporary victory of life, art, and morality over the vast force arrayed against it. The salmon was Wiener's hero.

One day as we sat in the luncheonette, where our conversations usually took place, Wiener predicted that within a decade or less, computers, which were then room-sized machines, would be miniaturized as solid-state devices replaced vacuum tubes. These miniaturized machines—he held out the palm of his hand to indicate their eventual size—would be linked by wireless or telephone lines to libraries and other sources of information so that everyone on earth could, in theory, have access to all but limitless data in an all-encompassing feedback loop, endlessly correcting and updating itself. Scientists, he said, would not have to wait months or years for journals to print their papers or commentators to reply but could communicate with their peers instantly. Moreover, dictators and censors could no longer control the flow of information. Reference materials could be stored and refreshed digitally and current data retrieved as needed. He predicted that reference books, which are out of date as soon as they are published, would no longer be supplied in bound volumes but would be kept up to date by new information from central data banks. He imagined a palimpsest of maps from ancient to modern on which human migrations and the rise and fall of civilizations could be traced.

What Wiener was predicting was the unmediated, open-ended seminar that seemed to me the ideal democracy. He was more optimistic than I am about human nature. He thought that a global feedback system might create a self-correcting human community. I thought it foreshadowed an intensified confrontation between the creative and destructive forces within human nature but we preferred not to debate these merely temperamental differences. The words "Internet" and "disintermediation," the latter made fashionable by a subsequent generation at MIT, had not yet been coined. But Wiener had foreseen their substance with characteristic insight and enthusiasm.

I dismissed this prophecy as science fiction, as I did another of Wiener's ideas that day: that human beings could be encoded, like any other collection of information, transmitted electronically at the speed of light, and decoded at the other end. In this way we could travel beyond the solar system. This, of course, actually did become a preoccupation of science fiction writers. But I should not have been so dismissive of his vision of linked computers. In the form of the World Wide Web these would eventually provide a solution to the overconcentrated retail book market which would soon preoccupy me. Moreover, by describing human beings as packets of information subject to decay in isolation, Wiener had provided a metaphor for the counterentropic value of interactivity as a source of cultural renewal.

My failure to take Wiener's prophecies seriously reflected the limitations of my own worldview at the time and that of my intellectual friends who were increasingly absorbed in Cold War issues and felt that the fate of Western civilization depended upon the positions they took in their articles for *Partisan Review* or in their dinner-party conversation. Unlike these friends, I had never been attracted to socialism, which presupposes an overoptimistic view of human nature and a premature answer to unanswerable questions. I agreed, however, with Marxists that technological changes—what Marx called changes in the forms of production—produce changes in consciousness. New industrial technologies in the early nineteenth century, for example, altered the relationship between craftsmen and their masters, who no longer worked together as colleagues but evolved into distinct classes of workers and owners in conflict. Marx's prophecy that this new class consciousness would lead to revolution, followed eventually by a workers' paradise, a wishful version of the Christian apocalypse, seemed to me foolish. But his idea that new technologies transform cultures seemed true even if his revolutionary fantasies did not. Movable type, after all, had enormous cultural consequences, and in the 1950s the literary culture was further transformed by the technology of internal combustion, which led to the suburban migration, the rise of the bookstore chains, and the dominance of commercial best-sellers at the expense of large, eccentric inventories. I should have seen that Wiener was describing an even more profound technological shift than either of these, but I had fallen under the spell of my New York friends. Because Wiener was not one of us, his prophecies seemed unreal to me and I ignored them.

By the time the Library of America appeared in the mid-eighties, Wiener had died and his prophecies were a distant memory. I had begun to hear about the Internet and companies called Compu-Serve and Prodigy from younger colleagues at

Random House, but their application to the book business did not occur to me. Had I been alert to these possibilities my next project might have turned out differently and perhaps disastrously.

The handful of first-rate independent book-stores strong enough to have survived into the mid-1980s were the last members of a species facing extinction. Elliott Bay in Seattle, Powell's in Port-land, Book Soup and Dutton's in Los Angeles, Black Oak and Cody's in the Bay Area, Books and Co. in Coral Gables, Coliseum in New York, Square Books in Oxford, Mississippi, the wonder-ful Northshire Books in Manchester, Vermont, were vigorous and well rooted in their habitats but unlikely to reproduce. Of this group, the most re-markable was Denver's Tattered Cover, whose forty thousand feet of retail space contained by the mid-1980s when I visited it many more than 100,000 titles in innumerable categories, many of which in-cluded everything in print on a given topic, titles so esoteric in some cases that it was impossible to imagine for whom they were written. Browsers could read at leisure in sofas and armchairs, and bright clerks remained out of sight until called upon. The children's department was like a one-room schoolhouse where children of various sizes sat on stools or on the floor reading. Denver had never been much of a book town, but the Tattered Cover had grown in twenty years or so from a typical side-street bookstore with a coy name into one of the great bookstores of the world. It had created a market for books that had never existed or been imaginable in Denver before.

The Tattered Cover showed that a potentially large audience existed for the myriad backlist books that could not be found in shopping malls at the time and that publishers were increasingly unable to keep in print. Moreover, Denver is a typical western city without a large university population or the bookish reputation of such cities as San Francisco and Boston. I wondered why, if the Tattered Cover flourished in Denver, its success couldn't be duplicated in other cities. One reason was obvious. The owner of the Tattered Cover is a marketing genius who chose to sell books rather than the more profitable goods to which other gifted marketers are drawn. Such talent devoted to books is uncommon. When I visited the original Borders store in Ann Arbor a few weeks later I learned that there was another reason that such stores may flourish under certain local conditions but not others.

Because of its university location, Borders

presented a more scholarly appearance than the Tattered Cover, but its categories were just as numerous and its inventory nearly as comprehensive. Unlike the Tattered Cover, Borders did not feature stacks of current best-sellers, but it displayed on a small shelf near the entrance a weekly selection of titles, new and old, obscure and current, that the staff thought might interest their customers. Otherwise the stock was displayed spine out on thousands of feet of shelves from which Joe Gable, the manager, who led me through the store, could select a title with his eyes shut. The Tattered Cover gave the impression of a magical book fair where every book in the world could be found simply by uttering the name of its author, but Borders was like the private library of a mythical polymath determined to devour all the knowledge in the world.

I visited Borders with my bookish friend Mort Zuckerman, who happened to be in the real estate business. My thought was that it might be possible to open a store like Borders or the Tattered Cover in New York, where nothing comparable had existed since Eighth Street closed ten years previously. To have flown with Mort to Denver for this purpose would have meant an overnight stay. A trip to Ann Arbor would answer our questions in an afternoon.

As it happened, our questions answered themselves when Tom Borders said that he needed more space but couldn't afford to rent the recently vacated area that occupied a corner of his own building and belonged to another owner. What Tom had acknowledged was the familiar trade-off between rent and inventory: high rent demands high turnover and high turnover requires best-sellers. The nature of Tom's inventory made it impossible for him to accept the trade-off demanded by the expensive additional space. I knew nothing about the financial structure of the Tattered Cover, but Denver at the time of my visit was in a real estate slump. The Tattered Cover was a mile or so beyond the downtown business district in a freestanding former department store. Obviously it was not paying New York rents, and neither was Borders. This helped explain their extensive inventories.

The prospect of maintaining vast inventories in expensive New York premises and hiring trained clerks at New York wages discouraged Mort and me from pursuing our idea. We felt that inevitably high-rent versions of the Tattered Cover or Borders in major cities would develop into mall stores on a larger scale, dependent on rates of turnover incompatible with very large, slow-moving invento-

ries. Moreover, we were not retailers, and operating a bookstore did not appeal to us. I decided
instead to create a virtual bookstore—the Tattered
Cover or Borders in the form of a direct-mail catalog, an annotated directory of thousands of backlist
titles that could be ordered by phone over a toll-
free number. The result a year later was *The Reader's
Catalog*, a two-thousand-page list of more than forty
thousand titles, as many as could be included in a
directory three inches thick.

Like Anchor Books and *The New York Review of
Books*, *The Reader's Catalog* was self-explanatory to the
audience for which it was intended, and copies sold
rapidly at $25. We linked our computer to that of a
national wholesaler from whose extensive inventories we filled orders within twenty-four hours and
soon discovered that a potentially vast worldwide
market existed for the great variety of backlist books
that could not be found in the mall stores and were
otherwise available only in the few large independent stores serving local markets to which most
Americans had no access. At first it appeared that
The Reader's Catalog would become a worldwide bookstore without walls offering an enormous range of
titles, eventually in all languages: in effect what
Amazon.com has become. But I had miscalculated:

I expected that the catalog could operate profitably on the 40 percent margin between what we paid the wholesaler and what we charged the customer together with the shipping and handling charges that the customer also paid. I was wrong. Though we shipped orders as soon as books arrived in our warehouse from the wholesaler, the handling costs, clerical salaries, and computer and credit card charges were more than I had budgeted for. I expected that as the business grew these costs as a percentage of sales would decline. Instead, as we added more staff to handle increased sales, I found that our margin would be insufficient no matter how the business grew even though we had the advantage of immediate payment from our customers and thirty days to pay our supplier and were increasingly ordering books directly from publishers at greater discounts.

The problem was not a matter of size. It was structural. Though we kept no inventories, had no retail premises, or salespeople and received payment in advance, a $25 or $30 average order simply did not produce enough margin to cover the cost of handling it and never would no matter how big the business became, for the more we grew the more infrastructure we would need to serve our expanding customer base. My predicament reminded me of the mess that a small-town druggist played by W. C. Fields had got himself into in a short film shot in the 1930s. To outflank the other drugstore in town, Fields offered free delivery night and day. Delighted with his strategy, he installed a phone and rubbed his hands in anticipation of the first order. Soon the phone rang and Fields could be heard repeating something like these instructions: "Turn left on Main Street and go ten miles, then turn right and follow a path into the woods until you come to a stream . . ." And then in a choked voice Fields asked, "And all you want is a two-cent stamp?" The economics of servicing inexpensive products had not changed since Fields's day. Meanwhile another problem arose that I had also failed to anticipate.

By the mid-1980s the mall chains had approached the limits of their expansion, and their original owners disposed of them. In 1984 Kmart bought Walden, and in 1986 Barnes & Noble bought B. Dalton. The new owners found not only that new locations were increasingly marginal but that sales in mature stores were leveling off so that the annual growth expected by investors could not be sustained. Meanwhile the Tattered Cover and other surviving independents had shown that extensive backlist inventories attract customers to large freestanding bookstores, which often cost less per square foot to occupy than comparable space in high-rent malls. Accordingly, the owners of the Walden chain acquired Borders, intending to replicate it nationally, while in 1989 Barnes & Noble bought Bookstop, a chain of large stores in the South modeled on the supermarket concept. This was the origin of the Barnes & Noble superstore chain. From the point of view of writers and readers, these superstores with their relatively large inventories were an improvement over the mall stores. But the price war in which the superstore chains immediately engaged meant that readers could now find the titles they wanted in *The Reader's Catalog* and order them at discounts from the chains. The catalog, whose margins were unsatisfactory in the first place, could not survive this competition. Eventually investors decided that the superstores could not survive their discount war either. By the first quarter of 2000 their share prices, having declined for months, had fallen to new lows.

Investors may have been discouraged further when the superstore chains, having expanded rapidly, saturated the limited locations where books can be sold and faced the same limits to future growth that their predecessors in the malls had faced when available locations became increasingly marginal. Meanwhile many of these superstores, under pressure to increase their margins, thinned their inventories, and, like the mall stores, featured current best-sellers and their own self-published editions of promotional titles, often, it seemed to me, at the expense of the strong backlist inventories that had been their original emphasis. This put them at a disadvantage compared to Internet retailers and supplied yet a third reason for investors to flee. The viability of the superstore chains, under pressure from Internet retailers and facing an even more severe electronic challenge in the future as authors and readers are linked electronically, is questionable. Meanwhile the chains, seeking to improve their fragile margins, exert increasing pressure on publishers to gamble on potential best-sellers and provide incentives that amount to additional discounts. Publishers and booksellers did not choose this dance of death, but neither partner can escape the other's embrace.

When I conceived *The Reader's Catalog* in the mid-1980s I arranged with Prodigy, an early and unsuccessful attempt to create an Internet shopping service, to feature it. Prodigy's strategy, however, was to become a virtual shopping mall. The engineers who created it did not understand that backlist was the catalog's strength and that the Internet's advantage over conventional retailers is its ability to market limitless, unconventional inventories serving a great variety of interests. Prodigy unwisely used *The Reader's Catalog* to promote only current best-sellers and the experiment predictably failed.

Meanwhile, individual publishers were creating their own Web sites but had only vague ideas of how to exploit them. The results were negligible. Publishers were reluctant to sell their titles directly to consumers in competition with retail booksellers even at full price, much less at competitive discounts. Moreover, readers were not interested in buying a Random House book or a HarperCollins book any more than filmgoers want to see a Paramount or Fox film. Publishers' experimental Web sites were an expensive dead end. As the success of the Tattered Cover showed, readers wanted a single comprehensive inventory from which to choose their books.

Amazon.com met this need by offering such an inventory over its own Web site, a decade after

Prodigy failed to do the same for *The Reader's Catalog*. But Amazon.com immediately encountered the structural problem of insufficient margin that *The Reader's Catalog* had faced and that dismayed W. C. Fields when he was asked to deliver a two-cent stamp. Moreover, Amazon.com was forced by competing Web sites to engage in suicidal price-cutting, from which the instantaneous price comparisons available on the Web offer no escape. Amazon.com was selling two-cent stamps at a 20 percent discount.

In the spring of 1997, Rea Hederman, the publisher of *The New York Review of Books*, who had taken charge of *The Reader's Catalog*, had just brought out a second edition. He and I had considered creating a Web site for the new edition but we abandoned the plan when Rea's business manager showed us that the Internet would not solve the structural problem of insufficient margin that defeated my previous attempt to operate the catalog as a virtual bookstore. Instead we decided to auction the right to use the catalog's updated annotated listings to an existing Internet retailer. The leading candidates were barnesandnoble.com and Amazon.com, and in April we met with Jeff Bezos, Amazon's founder, at my apartment in New York. We were candid with Bezos. We would be delighted to work with him, we told him, if he won the auction, but we also showed him the results of my initial attempt to sell books from *The Reader's Catalog* using a toll-free number and the even worse projections made by Rea's business manager if we now turned to the Internet. Bezos brushed these numbers aside and said that according to his projections, he would cover his fixed costs when his sales reached $200 million. Like me when I conceived *The Reader's Catalog* a decade earlier, Bezos did not see that he was committed to an incorrect business model, one in which costs would rise in proportion to sales while margins would remain under constant pressure from competitive discounts and high service costs.

Three years after this meeting, Amazon.com had lost nearly $900 million, a forgivable performance perhaps for promising start-up companies in today's hyperactive economy, but a catastrophic loss for what remains essentially a retail bookstore with sidelines in music, toys, electronic gadgets, drugstore items, and so on. E-commerce is not exempt from the rules of cost accounting. Sears and Wal-Mart began as structurally sound small retailers and maintained their profitability as they grew. The structural problems of online retailers, by contrast, are intrinsic and cannot be outgrown. Online commerce rewards unmediated transactions between producer and consumer. It abhors middlemen, a vestige of earlier and obsolete technologies, and devours their cash. In 1999, Amazon's chief competitor, barnesandnoble.com, lost $102 million on sales of $202 million, the point at which Bezos had told Rea Hederman and me that he planned to break even, while Amazon.com itself lost $719 million on sales of $1.63 billion. Amazon combined the announcement of its loss for 1999 with the good news that its bookselling business would break even in the following quarter, but this prophecy may have anticipated the reallocation of overhead costs from books to other low-margin Amazon product lines rather than enhanced overall cash flow.

Perhaps Amazon.com will evolve into another kind of business, a brokerage for a variety of goods and services or an advertising medium. Perhaps it will be become an online distributor of electronic texts. As its losses grew, there was talk of "leveraging its customer base," jargon for selling access to its millions of customers to sellers of other products. But Amazon's book buyers may not be equally interested in other products while Amazon's affiliated retailers will face the same low margins that afflict

Amazon itself. Like Fields's pharmacy, Amazon.com has acquired a customer base by selling goods and providing services at a loss. But its customer base is volatile, free to leave in an electronic instant should another retailer offer better service and even lower prices or should Amazon.com itself conclude that it can no longer afford to support customers who demand goods and services for which they are not asked to pay.

It was obvious to many in the industry by 1998 that Amazon could not overcome the structural problems that defeated *The Reader's Catalog*. But a possible alternative was also obvious. If publishers formed a consortium to sell their books directly to readers over the Internet, the logic of Internet marketing, to which middlemen are extraneous, would be acknowledged and the problem of insufficient margin would be overcome. What I had in mind was a consortium open to all publishers, old and new, large and small, on equal terms. This consortium would create a combined annotated catalog of all its titles and maintain warehouses where books from diverse publishers would be packed and shipped directly to Internet buyers. The elimination of wholesalers and retailers would permit the consortium's component publishers to reduce prices to consumers, pay higher royalties to writers, and increase their own margins. To the extent that books are sold by the consortium directly to consumers, the problem of returns from overstocked retailers would also be eliminated.

The concept of such a consortium was simple. To implement it proved impossible. Though the Internet made such a consortium sooner or later inevitable, the conglomerate managers to whom I presented the idea were not enthusiastic, nor was Jeff Bezos when I suggested to him that a solution to his problem of insufficient margin might be to convert Amazon from a retailer to a brokerage, transmitting orders for a fee to a publishers' consortium, if one could be arranged.

An immediate objection to my plan by the publishers to whom I presented it was the likely reaction of retailers, but other obstacles were less tangible and probably more decisive. These overseas managers were not themselves book publishers and had not experienced the devolution of the American industry and its retail marketplace. The more naive ones were fixated on best-sellers and underestimated the value of backlists. All of them were preoccupied with navigating the obsolete and unseaworthy vessels they had recently acquired past uncharted reefs in unfamiliar waters. Though a publishers' consortium was an obvious strategy, tactically it required the daring and finesse of Lord Nelson. A counterattack from booksellers, for example, was inevitable, but the consortium could argue that direct selling by publishers would not increase the market share of online retailing beyond what Amazon.com and barnesandnoble.com had already achieved. On the other hand, the consortium would make online bookselling a viable business, one that Amazon.com and its Internet competitors could profitably serve as brokers. But adroit maneuvers were too much to expect of overworked managers patching sails, plugging leaks, and hoping not to be pitched overboard while learning port from starboard.

New technologies create appropriate infrastructure. An annotated universal catalog of digitized titles that can be downloaded in various forms is an essential component of future Internet bookselling. So are machines that can reliably and cheaply print one book at a time in remote locations according to a customer's request. These new technologies will not, in my opinion, preclude retail bookstores. Shops like the Tattered Cover and Northshire or the surviving chain store branches will flourish for the same reasons that cinemas flourish despite television and videotapes. New technologies do not erase the past, but build upon it.

The old histories of East Hampton mention a silver-voiced peddler named Mason Locke Weems who had once been a preacher and still called himself Parson. On an autumn day not long after the death of President Washington in 1799, Weems rode into this highly literate Long Island village with a drum strapped to his back. He placed himself under one of the great elms that lined the village green, un-limbered his drum, and after a few thumps had at-tracted a crowd. It was probably a Philadelphia printer named John Ormrod who now and then took to the road as a bookseller who had told Weems that Federalist East Hampton was a good market for the book he was planning to write about George Washington. In the previous year, Weems and Ormrod had been hired to sell subscriptions to the five-volume life of Washington written by John Marshall, the great third Chief Justice, and his fel-low jurist the President's favorite nephew, Bushrod Washington. Ormrod had been assigned the Northern states and Weems had been asked to drum up business in the much less promising Anti-

Federalist South. Now Weems had come north to Federalist East Hampton to find subscribers for his own, mostly fictional life of Washington with its cherry tree and hatchet and dollar thrown across the Rappahanock.

Weems did not need a publisher to sell his book on the East Hampton village green. He publicized and sold his book himself, covering his costs and earning his profit directly from future readers who would eventually be sent their copies by post. Perhaps Weems also relied on these future readers for editorial help, taking note of the inventions they liked and shaping his book accordingly. When Weems visited East Hampton the publishing industry in the United States had not yet been born. There were printers in the important towns and cities, but East Hampton had no bookseller. Like Weems, many writers in those days either sold their books themselves—according to Marshall's biographer, Weems was a storyteller who could charm an audience with the fiddle as well as the drum—or if they lacked Weems's magnetism they arranged with others to do the job for them, as John Marshall and Bushrod Washington did when they hired a Federalist newspaper publisher in Richmond who in turn hired Ormrod and Weems to go on the road.*

Soon writers and readers will be able to meet again on a worldwide village green where writers may once more beat their drums or hire a Weems to drum up business for them. On the World Wide Web, future storytellers and their readers can mingle at leisure and talk at length. Writers of cookbooks, garden books, regional guides, and other reference books and directories can, if they like, compose their texts interactively with their future readers, as Weems probably did with his. So may poets and other storytellers, who will find at the end of the process that buyers, identifiable by their e-mail addresses, await the finished work in either printed or electronic form or in forms yet to be

---

* More than a good salesman, Weems was wise to the future of publishing. In a January 22, 1797, letter to Matthew Carey, a bookman in Philadelphia for whom he acted as agent, Weems predicted the paperback revolution: "Experience has taught me that small, i.e. quarter of a dollar books, on subjects calculated to strike the popular curiosity, printed in very large numbers and properly distributed, would prove an immense revenue to the prudent and industrious undertakers." (From M. L. Weems, *The Life of Washington*, edited by Marcus Cunliffe, Harvard University Press, 1962. The author's thanks to Hugh Rawson for providing the story.)

devised. But guides, directories, catalogs, almanacs, and so on, which are out of date on the day they are published, need never be printed at all. Instead, their data can be continuously updated and retrieved electronically as needed.

The best advertising for any book is word of mouth. For this the global village green offers limitless scope. But the Web will be more than a platform from which books are promoted and sold. Some books will be composed interactively on the Web and others will be compiled to order from random sources and delivered electronically in a single package or in periodic revisions. Employees transferred to new locations in Seattle, Nairobi, Taipei, or Poughkeepsie can be given compilations from several sources by their companies on local conditions, history, and facilities and access to a Web site that will answer additional questions as they arise. Interactive curricula can be transmitted from a single site to students in distant places. So can medical, legal, and financial advice be addressed interactively to individual users. For historians and other scholars the prospects of multidimensional research are beguiling. With books no longer imprisoned for life within fixed bindings the opportunities are endless for the creation of new, useful, and profitable products by Internet publishers. For Walt Whitman and his ever-changing editions of *Leaves of Grass* the Web would have been ideal. So would it have been for Theodore Dreiser and Vladimir Nabokov, plagued with squeamish and ignorant publishers, as it would also have been for samizdat writers in the former Soviet Union and will be for their counterparts under today's tyrannies.

Among the many tyrannies to be overcome by the World Wide Web will be the turnover requirements of retail booksellers. On the infinitely expandable shelves of the World Wide Web, there will be room for a virtually limitless variety of books that can be printed on demand or reproduced on hand-held readers or similar devices. The invention of movable type created opportunities for writers that could not be anticipated in Gutenberg's day. The opportunities that await writers and their readers in the near future are immeasurably greater.

The obstacles imposed between readers and writers by traditional publishing practices—a system of improvisations accumulated over generations from the vagaries and impasses of obsolete technologies—will wither away. The global village green will not be paradise. It will be undisciplined, poly-morphous, and polyglot, as has been our fate and our milieu ever since the divine autocracy showed its muscle by toppling the monolingual Tower of Babel. Over the objections of countless local gods and their vicars, writers have ever since improvised many imperfect towers of their own—clearings in the forest, marketplaces in Athens, catacombs in Rome, graffiti on dungeon walls, samizdat in Siberian camps—and they will do so hereafter with unprecedented scope on the World Wide Web. On this point, there are strong grounds for optimism. The critical faculty that selects meaning from chaos is part of our instinctual equipment, and so is the gift for creating and recreating civilizations and their rules without external guidance. Human be-ings have a genius for finding their way, for creat-ing goods, making orderly markets, distinguishing quality, and assigning value. This faculty can be taken for granted. There is no reason to fear that the awesome diversity of the World Wide Web will overwhelm it. In fact, the Web's diversity will en-large these powers, or so one's experience of hu-mankind permits one to hope.

Whether publishers adapt to this opportunity with foresight or leave it to others is unclear. What is clear is that on the World Wide Web, publishers' tasks can be reduced to an essential handful: editorial support, publicity, design, digitizing, and financing. For these functions, size confers no advantage and at a certain magnitude becomes a nuisance. My guess is that future publishing units will be small, though they may be related to a central financial source. To the extent that writers deliver the contents of their minds directly to the minds of their readers over the Web, as Stephen King has done, such vestigial publishing work as marketing, sales, shipping, and warehousing together with their bureaucracies and inefficiencies can be minimized and assigned to specialist firms. Book publishing may therefore become once more a cottage industry of diverse, creative autonomous units, or so there is now reason to believe.

Index

BOOK

BUSINESS

Publishing

Past Present and Future

By Jason Epstein

For information about permission to reproduce selections from
this book, write to Permissions, W. W. Norton & Company, Inc.,
500 Fifth Avenue, New York, NY 10110.

The text of this book is composed in Mrs Eaves Roman
with the display set in Mrs Eaves Petite Caps
Desktop composition by Molly Heron
Manufacturing by The Haddon Craftsmen, Inc.
Book design by Rubina Yeh

Library of Congress Cataloging-in-Publication Data

Epstein, Jason.
Book business : publishing past, present, and future / by Jason Epstein.
p.   cm.
Includes index.
ISBN 0-393-04984-1
1. Publishers and publishing—History—20th century. 2. Publishers
and publishing—Forecasting. 3. Epstein, Jason. I. Title.
Z280 .E67 2001
070.5'09—dc21   00-060079

W. W. Norton & Company, Inc.,
500 Fifth Avenue, New York, NY 10110
www.wwnorton.com

W. W. Norton & Company Ltd.,
10 Coptic Street, London WC1A 1PU

1   2   3   4   5   6   7   8   9   0

To
Judith Miller

The most primitive idols, even those which have long been abandoned to the jungle and the sand-drift, are land-marks in the journey of the human soul: they represent a search for coherence in the confusions and fears of living. So this venerable House of Lords was not simply a constitutional relic of the great landed fortunes; it was also a fetish, it meant the ideally paternal responsibility of the noble few. And though this meaning was quite irrel-evant to the twentieth century yet those who tried to preserve it were not merely idle or arrogant men. They saw the passing of certain values which at their best were very high and at their worst were very human; they did not realize that life consists in change, that nothing can stand still, that today's shrines are only fit for tomorrow's cattle. Clinging to the realities of the past, they prepared to defend their dead cause to the finish.

George Dangerfield, *The Strange Death of Liberal England*